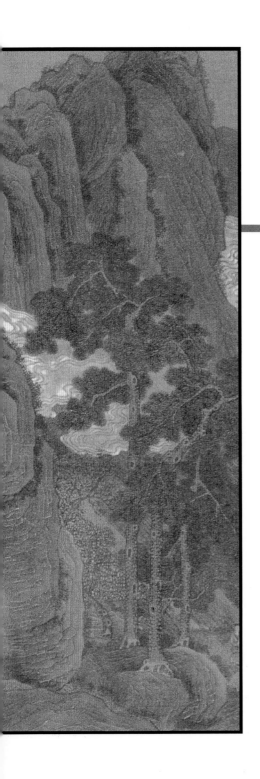

THE
PERSONAL
FENG SHUI
MANUAL

*How to develop a healthy
and harmonious
lifestyle*

MASTER LAM KAM CHUEN

An Owl Book
Henry Holt and Company
New York

Henry Holt and Company, Inc.
Publishers since 1866
115 West 18th Street
New York, New York 10011

Henry Holt ® is a registered
trademark of Henry Holt and Company, Inc.

First published in the United States in 1998
by Henry Holt and Company, Inc.

Published in Canada by Fitzhenry & Whiteside Ltd.,
195 Allstate Parkway, Markham, Ontario L3R 4T8.

Originally published in the United Kingdom in 1998
by Gaia Books Ltd.

Library of Congress Cataloging-in-Publication Data
available on request

ISBN 0-8050-5558-4

Henry Holt books are available for special promotions and
premiums. For details contact: Director, Special Markets.

First American Edition – 1998

Printed and bound in Singapore.
All first editions are printed on acid-free paper. ∞

10 9 8 7 6 5 4 3 2 1

FRONTISPIECE *Landscape in blue and
green painted in ink and colors on silk
by Zhao Boju (early 12th century)*

Contents

Introduction

Why is it that we feel nervous and ill at ease when we sit on a stool in the middle of a crowded room? Why do almost all cultures punish children by making them face the wall in a corner?

Why do we have a sudden rush of comfort and power when we sit in a large chair with a high back and wide arms? Why do certain colors attract us while others make us wary?

Why is it that one home seems perfectly suited to one family yet disastrous for another? Are these experiences common to everyone or do they happen only to some of us?

There was a time when such questions could be dismissed as idle curiosity. But with the growing interest throughout the world in the art of Feng Shui (pronounced "fung shoy"), people are waking up to the fact that these puzzles have been the subject of painstaking examination by oriental scholars for centuries – and that the answers can make a great difference to our daily lives.

At the same time, many people are bewildered by the array of available books on Feng Shui. Some are by Chinese authors, some by Western writers. The information in them seems contradictory and the hope of finding quick and easy interior design solutions suddenly fades.

But the hunger for a practical introduction to the fundamental principles of this art has not gone away. That perhaps accounts for the warmth with which Gaia's first book on this subject, *The Feng Shui Handbook*, was greeted. Since it appeared in 1995, it has been extensively reprinted and widely translated.

The Personal Feng Shui Manual is a companion volume. It is designed to be read independently; at the same time, readers of *The Feng Shui Handbook* will immediately find that it builds on the basic principles set out there and leads them further in their understanding of Feng Shui. It shows how those fundamental principles can be applied to their own personal circumstances.

Understanding energy

Every human being lives under the influence of two immense fields of energy. Below us is the constant power of the Earth. Above us, and extending through the immeasurable vastness of space, is the energy of the cosmos.

Understanding the influence of these energies, and their impact on the lives of individuals, is the basis of Feng Shui. The Chinese characters for Feng Shui themselves stand for Wind and Water, both forms of vital energy – one visible, one invisible – on which most life forms depend for their existence.

Although the term Feng Shui is now the common description of the study of all such energies, the origins of this natural science, in fact, go back much farther in the history of Chinese culture. The ancients referred to their explorations of energy as Ham Yu. These two characters convey an extremely sophisticated, intuitive understanding of the position of the human being in the universe.

The Chinese character Ham literally means "looking into the heavens", Yu means "looking at the earth". This is the image evoked by the photograph on the cover of this book and opposite – the human being, a creature of the earth, yet, with each step, striding through the universe.

Ham

Yu

The heavens, humans, and the earth

The ancient understanding of the universe was skilfully expressed by the combination of simple brush strokes in early Chinese calligraphy. The three characters that represent the heavens, the human being, and the earth offer one of the most illuminating ways of understanding our situation in the cosmos.

We begin with the two brush strokes that represent the human being. This is the ideogram (Yun). It is perhaps the simplest of all images: a creature who is erect and walking forward.

The next character, for the heavens, consists of four brush strokes. This is the ideogram (Tin), often translated simply as Heaven. You can see that it includes the two brush strokes for the human being. Then there is one horizontal stroke immediately above the person and one crossing in the middle. The smaller of the two horizontal lines stands for the moon and the longer one is for the sun. These in turn correspond to the classical lines used to denote the two fundamental forces of Yin and Yang (pages 12–13).

The third character is the earth, drawn with five brush strokes. This is the ideogram (Dih). At the bottom is a long line for the earth. On the left hand is a single vertical line with a small horizontal line crossing it. This denotes something sticking into the earth or perhaps growing out of it, like a tree. This literally conveys the meaning "mud". The three strokes to the right represent a utensil, a tool, possibly a farm implement such as a plough, conveying the idea of things being used. Taken altogether the five strokes express the idea of "the land".

Here is an entire way of seeing ourselves expressed in eleven brush strokes. It lies at the

The human being: a walking figure, upright, like an antenna moving between the powerful forces of the earth below and the heavens above.

Heaven consists of two powers, the sun and moon, the great forces of Yin and Yang, having a direct relationship to the energy of the human being who moves between them.

This is the earth: the land, useful and fertile mud, tilled by implements, giving birth to all that grows out of it, and accepting everything that descends into it.

heart of all authentic Feng Shui. For Feng Shui draws together a range of closely interconnected systems for examining and interpreting the relationship between the energies of the earth, the energies of the galaxies, and the energy patterns of each individual human being.

Your innermost motivations
Feng Shui is a vast field of study and an accomplished master of this art would normally be expected to have undertaken some thirty years of study and practice under one or more masters, possibly specialising in different aspects such as time cycles or architectural design. So it is not possible for one book to convey more than a fingernail's worth of the subject matter encompassed by this remarkable scholarship.

This book will help you understand two aspects of the heaven–human–earth relationship. First, there is the relationship between your own energies and those which affect you by virtue of your birth at a particular time in the life of the universe. This is encoded in considerable detail in the workings of Chinese astrology, of which a full explanation would itself take several volumes.

As a first step, however, Part One gives you a description of the distinctive qualities of the human spirit which are characteristic of a person born at any point in the twelve-year cycles of the Chinese Zodiac. Carefully studied, these small portraits open doors to some of your innermost motivations, revealing how you approach a subject like Feng Shui and how you see your environment, friends, and work. It also provides information that you can use in other practical ways such as preparing for job interviews, described later in

the book. Armed with this awareness of your own energetic properties, you are better able to use your inner power in conjunction with the energy of rooms, spaces, and other people to affect important moments in your life.

Fields of energy
The second aspect of the heaven–human–earth relationship which you will learn about is a method for establishing whether your own field of energy is compatible with that of any house, flat, or apartment you might want to make your home. Using an ordinary compass, together with the charts and Feng Shui "tools" in Part One, you are provided with a complete system in itself, which also tells you your individual relationship to significant numerals in Chinese numerology and to the colors of The Five Energies.

Part Two then shows how to understand the flows of energy in everyday situations, often combined with information about The Five Energies (see pages 10–11), so that you can create secure, positive environments for yourself or others wherever you are. This can apply to choosing a chair in a room on the basis of its shape, its location, its color, and its compatibility with your own energy field. Or arranging the family dinner table. Or deciding where to sit in a cinema or restaurant.

It also examines similar problems in the work environment: the layout of offices and meeting rooms and understanding the nature of pervasive, electromagnetic environments.

The Five Energies

The study of the movement of energy forms the basis of one of the most famous analytical systems in Chinese culture – Wu Hsing. The phrase is often translated as The Five Elements, but it can be better understood as The Five Energies. It is based on the fact that energy tends to move in five directions: radiating outwards, concentrating inwards, rising and descending, and rotating.

Wu

Hsing

In the system of The Five Energies, different colors, smells, and tastes are seen as manifestations of each of these energies. So are the seasons, foods, directions, and numbers. All these phenomena, which are often mistakenly viewed as inanimate and static, are understood in Feng Shui to be vibrations in a vast dance of energy.

The Five Energies are described using the names of five natural phenomena which typify those movements of energy: Fire, Earth, Metal, Water, and Wood.

Fire energy shoots upward. It is energy at its peak, like the full moon, brilliant and full. Earth energy moves around its own axis and affects the period of change between each of the seasons. Earth energy corresponds to that phase of the moon when it is full, golden, and closest to the Earth just before it wanes. Metal energy moves inward, becoming ever more dense. It is likened to the waning moon. Water energy descends; it occupies the point in the cycle (see page 11) of maximum rest. It is the new moon, dark and about to give birth. Wood symbolizes expanding energy, growing outward like a tree. It is the beginning of growth, the waxing moon.

The Five Energies have an impact far beyond themselves. They interact with each other in cyclical patterns. Each energy is preceded by another, known as its "parent", and is followed by its "child".

The circle of The Five Energies on the facing page reveals an interdependent relationship. Begin with Fire at the top and move back to Wood. Wood is the parent of Fire. Earth is the child of Fire. At the same time, Earth is the parent of Metal, the next energy in the cycle. Metal is the child of Earth and the parent of Water – Water, the child of Metal, is the parent of Wood. Wood, the child of Water, becomes the parent of Fire.

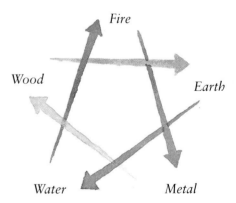

The Five Energies control each other through a relationship known as the Control Cycle. Fire controls Metal. If Fire is too powerful, Metal loses its power. Earth controls Water. If Earth is too strong, it impedes the natural energy of Water. Metal controls Wood. If Metal is overpowering, it may harm Wood. Water controls Fire. If Water is too forceful, it may extinguish Fire. Wood controls Earth. If Wood is too expansive, it disturbs Earth energy.

The ancient way

To see the world through the eyes of a Feng Shui practitioner is to experience yourself constantly moving through a vast field of interrelated movements of energy. This world view is remarkably consistent with the most highly evolved speculations and discoveries of late 20th-century science. But it has its roots in a contemplative tradition of understanding nature that stretches back thousands of years to the agrarian society of early Chinese civilization.

Any authentic Feng Shui master must have a deep understanding of that tradition and two of its most remarkable fruits. The great *I Ching* (pronounced "ee ching"), widely known as *The Book of Changes*, describes basic patterns of energetic transformation. It is used by a Feng Shui master to determine the likely course of events that will flow from the configurations of converging energy fields (such as the coinciding energies of individual people at certain times in specific places). The Feng Shui tools in Part One of this book are drawn directly from the *I Ching* (see pages 64–83).

The Tao (pronounced "dow") is the other extraordinary realization to emerge from the scholars of Ancient China. Its meaning is as simple as it is mysterious: The Way. The phrase has become increasingly familiar outside China through the many translations of the *Tao Teh Ching* (pronounced "dow deh ching"). The profound philosophy of this slim volume lies at the heart of the art of Feng Shui. Ascribed to the sage Lao Tse, which means simply "Old Master", its intuitive poetry describes an unfolding world in which most conventional logic dissolves. Where the *I Ching* follows a strict logic of cause and effect, the Tao embraces this but is entirely at home with other ways of seeing connections between apparently unconnected phenomena:

Out of the Tao emerges the One.
Out of the One, comes Two.
Two gives birth to Three.
Everything else comes from Three.

Encoded in these lines is the underlying model of the Feng Shui universe. Everything (our bodies, our thoughts, our experiences, and all that we encounter as we live) arises from the energetic potential of the universe, the Tao. Like a description of the immeasurable field of energy from which we find the smallest waves and particles emerging, the *Tao Teh Ching* describes the Tao in these words:

It is beyond form,
It is beyond sound,
It is intangible.

Within the Tao is the primal energy, known in Chinese as Wu Chi – like the invisible, awesome power that gathers in storm clouds long before they shake the earth with their thunderbolts. This is The One.

From that raw, pregnant energy come the fundamental forces of Yin and Yang, the mother and father of all transformation. These are The Two.

The interaction of these two polar forces, the ceaseless interaction of Yin and Yang, makes Three. And from that chemistry the entire display of the world is born.

Thus, the *Tao Teh Ching* tells us in words that have great meaning for the Feng Shui practitioner:

All things arise from the Tao –
They are formed out of Matter,
They are shaped by their environment.

This principle provides the foundation for the use of the Feng Shui tools given to you in Part One of this book. For example, supposing you are considering moving into a new house and you decide to examine it from a Feng Shui point of view. The earth on which the house stands and the house itself are regarded as Yin. They are both still, "formed out of matter". The energy that surrounds the house and comes to it from the galaxy is Yang. It is in motion: it follows the unfolding of space and the cycles of time. When the house is closed, the Yin energy is inside and the Yang energy is outside. There is no interaction. But when the house is opened, the two energies interact, "shaped by their environment".

At the same time, the human being enters the home, bringing to the equation the additional variables of his or her own energy patterns. These patterns, too, are formed out of matter and are shaped by their environment. And so a further reaction is initiated between the changing energies of the house, the forces of the universe at that moment, and the specific polarities of the person. The reactions will be different for each person. But, equally, the energetic properties that the person manifests will be shaped by the conditions in which they find themselves. In the words of the old saying: "A tiger is Yang when it is awake, but Yin when it sleeps."

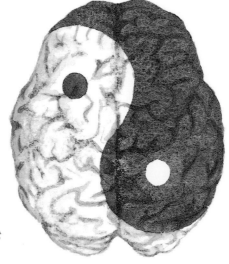

Yin and Yang are two powers. Both have immense potential, just like the positive and negative poles of an electrical field. Neither is more important or more powerful than the other. Like the two halves of the human brain, each manifests an essential quality and both are necessary in the full display of our potential.

Neither is fully dominant. One side of the brain seems to direct the powers of logic, mathematics, and manipulation; the other side works with the powers of intuition and creative association. Each is in a constantly changing relationship of perfect, simultaneous communication: both stimulating and controlling, energizing and pacifying.

Markets

Marketplaces continue to be one of the great meeting points of humanity. Many are modern shopping centers and, seen through the eyes of a Feng Shui master, some are far more successful than others.

The famed Galeries Lafayette in Paris (left) is a splendid example of the ability of buildings to attract energy. The soaring, circular interior enables energy to circulate freely, imbuing the visitor with feelings of freedom, heightened energy, and delight. The lines of the upper tiers resemble open wings and the topmost galleries are like eyelids lifting to receive the light that streams in through the glass dome.

The design of a successful shopping mall, according to Feng Shui principles, will be one in which energy is able to float or spin gently around the interior. If it is designed like a tunnel (right), incoming energy will simply enter at one end and leave through the other, encouraging people to pass quickly past the shops. This ornate arcade in London is often used by busy locals simply as a short-cut between two streets.

The huge Eaton Center in downtown Toronto, with its myriad curves and circles, conforms to many Feng Shui principles. Even the corners of the steps are rounded, creating harmonious movements of energy. In the far distance a hanging sculpture shows a flight of geese landing, just as the energy which descends into this space is welcomed and allowed to move calmly within.

Reflections

This is a book of mirrors – at least six of them. What is seen in the mirrors remains constant: you and your immediate surroundings. But each mirror offers you a slightly different view of who you are and where you are. It is a little like being inside a hexagon of full length reflectors – at each turn you see yourself from a different angle as well as reflections from the other mirrors.

What are these six mirrors? The first two are the Tao and the theory of Yin and Yang, whose essence is described on pages 12 and 13. Properly understood, these treasures of Chinese philosophy begin to change our perception of everything, transforming our understanding of fixed entities into an endless procession of changing forces.

Then comes the Chinese Zodiac to which you are introduced on pages 22–49. According to your year of birth, you find that you are likely to have certain inner qualities which influence your perceptions and behaviours. Those properties are part of the energetic pattern of being who you are.

Then there are the eight trigrams of the *I Ching* (pages 64–83) which apply the wisdom of *The Book of Changes* to your life, according to the year of your birth. Here is a different view, telling you in which direction favourable energies arise. An example of how to use that information in your office arrangement is given on pages 128–9.

Coupled with the information about the trigrams is another mirror, The Five Energies (pages 10–11, 64–83). You are told which of those energies is fundamental to you, which

others support you, and which ones tend to be in conflict with you. An example of how to use this is "Power seating" on pages 94–5.

Finally, most of Part Two is devoted to providing you with a further mirror: a personal view finder based on the template of the Five Animals so that you can always assess the energetic properties of your own location, regardless of where you are sitting, what you are facing, or what is unfolding around you.

Beyond that, there are further mirrors – not for you, but for the places where you live, work, and enjoy yourself. These include the circles you use to determine the principal direction of any property (pages 50–61) and the aspects you should consider in places such homes, offices, and public places.

Feng Shui in practice
At first, this profusion of mirrors can seem confusing. If you are looking for a simple way of seeing everything, especially yourself, then it can be baffling to be told: "Here are several different views of your identity; each varies, each is valid, all of them are you."

Confusion can turn to disappointment. You may have been led to believe that Feng Shui is a rigid system or, as people are fond of saying, an exact science. In that case, you might expect to be told "If you were born in 1958, you will definitely have good luck this year" or "Always put a goldfish bowl in the south-west corner of your front room and you will be rich." Whatever this sort of mindless instruction is, it definitely has no bearing on authentic Feng Shui.

The idea of an exact, prescriptive science – like all interpretations of our world – relies on a certain view of the way things are. If the world is filled with fixed entities, predictable forces, and experiments that will always produce the same results under scrupulously controlled conditions, then an exact science will inevitably be one capable of making certain types of accurate predictions.

However, the world is not fixed. It is subject to a larger range of influences, many of them uncontrollable and capable of exerting power over vast distances. It is a world in which the human being is a powerful, active element in the chemistry of energetic reactions. And so the very nature of what we mean by exact science changes. In such a world, an "exact" science is more person-centered. It offers a description of likely interactions between people and the complex forces that surround them. Its exactitude is rooted in the highly specific circumstances of each person. It works with a larger number of variables and takes greater account of the unpredictable.

This was the world vision of the ancients as they developed the natural science of Ham Yu (page 6), the ancestor of Feng Shui. They saw the sky as Yang – full of energy in the winds, the drifting clouds, the life-giving properties of the air itself. Below was the Earth, completely stable in relation to the moving atmosphere around it, solid, nurturing, and protective, a source of irresistible energy in itself. This was the power of Yin. Between these two lived the human family, with its own energetic properties, affected by everything around it, and constantly at work, changing the world.

Oddly enough, for all its emphasis on immaterial forces, Feng Shui has evolved into an extraordinarily practical field of study. Using this book as your personal Feng Shui manual, you will be able to identify and solve a range of common everyday problems, improve your life at home and at work, and increase the positive energy in your life.

On a deeper level, you may find that the pages of this book lead you to more profound observations as you see yourself and your world reflected in their manifold mirrors. Although still elementary by Feng Shui standards, they offer glimpses of a truly extraordinary world.

The house is silent.
The door is closed.
A person enters.
The window is opened wide.
Yang enters the Yin.
A baby is born.

*View of a garden, painted in ink and colors
on paper by Tang Yifen (1778–1853)*

PART ONE

The Essential Qualities

The essential qualities

Each moment in time and every point in space has its own essential quality. A Feng Shui master is trained to detect these qualities and to interpret the consequences of the relations between them.

You, too, possess essential qualities in your spirit and your personal energy patterns. You are born with these qualities and they remain with you throughout your life.

These inborn qualities are part of the inheritance you acquire as a result of being born at a particular time in the life cycles of the universe. Understanding the impact of these unfolding cycles is part of the extensive field of study embraced by Feng Shui.

The Chinese Zodiac

One aspect of Feng Shui wisdom is conveyed through the Chinese Zodiac, which deals with the first part of the trio of relationships between heaven, humans, and the earth (see pages 8–9). The Zodiac can be thought of as a mirror which reflects the relationship of cosmic energies (Heaven) to each person (Human).

As you will see from the following pages, your particular energies are characterized in the Zodiac by one of 12 animals. Your place in the Zodiac is determined by your date of birth. For example, using the chart on pages 24–5, you will find that if you were born between 10 February 1948 and 28 January 1949, your energies are symbolized by the Rat. You can then read about the inherent energies of such people on pages 26–7.

These energies take shape in the way you perceive and behave in the world. They are the foundations of some of the most powerful aspects of your personality. They include qualities such as persistence, sensitivity, and adaptability. You can think of these as patterns of mental or psychic energy, acting like carrier waves for other frequencies. For example, an underlying quality of persistence helps keep our intellectual, emotional, and physical energies from flagging. If we have a deep-seated sensitivity, this will be reflected in the feelings and thoughts we have towards others and our way of noticing our environment. If we are born with a quality of fundamental adaptability, this will help determine our response to all events, both psychological and physical.

I Ching

A second mirror in which you can see other aspects of your fundamental energy is the system of trigrams in the *I Ching*, *The Book of Changes* (see pages 64–83). The particular trigram to which you correspond is also determined by your date of birth.

For example, if you were born between 10 February 1948 and 28 January 1949, your corresponding energy is that of Lake (if you are male) or Mountain (if you are female). You can then read about the inherent energies of such people on pages 70–1 (Lake) or 80–1 (Mountain).

The particular energies described by the *I Ching* are different to those in the Zodiac, but they are also fundamental to your way of being in the world. In each of the descriptions of the trigrams you are told which of the patterns in the system of The Five Energies you manifest. Thus, if your trigram is Lake, your energy is that of Metal, and if your trigram is Mountain, your energy is that of Earth. Taken together, the descriptions will give you a composite portrait of the energy patterns that you embody in your life.

The Feng Shui Circles

This first part of the book also provides you with a basic understanding of the relationship between your essential qualities and the inherent energies of any place in which you wish to live. The method for doing this is first to determine which of the eight Feng Shui Circles on pages 54–61 corresponds to the property you are examining. Any such place has a center and a principal direction. Determining that direction is the first step in knowing whether you will be compatible with the property. You will discover how to determine that direction using the Feng Shui tools on pages 50–1.

The Ba Kua

Next, and equally importantly, you will learn how to establish your own Ba Kua – the classical eight-sided representation of your trigram. The eight Ba Kua are shown on pages 68–83. Your individual Ba Kua is automatically provided on the page that faces your trigram, which you have selected using the chart of years on pages 66–7.

Knowing your Ba Kua has many uses. First of all, you can determine whether its energy patterns match those of the Feng Shui Circle for the property you are examining. The method for determining this is explained on pages 50–1.

The information about your own Ba Kua also tells you about your relationship to the system of The Five Energies and the directions from which energies may arise – these can affect you positively or negatively. With this initial knowledge of your personal Feng Shui, you will be equipped to explore and cope with the range of auspicious or inauspicious circumstances detailed in Part Two.

Directions

The Feng Shui tools you are given in this part of the book pay considerable attention to the direction in which energy flows and your relationship to it. For example, if your Ba Kua is that of Earth, you may be advised that auspicious energy will arise in the South West and the North East. You may also benefit from energy from the West and the North West. But you should be cautious about energy flowing from the North, South, East, and South East. So, using this advice, you can then check the positions of any doors on your property that face an inauspicious direction and make sure they are closed except when in use.

Colors and numbers

Your trigram will also provide practical advice about favourable and unfavourable colors and numbers. Some colors complement your internal energy and so are best suited to you; others may have a negative effect and should be used sparingly or not at all. Try to apply the advice to all areas of your life, from clothing to interior decorating.

For example, if your trigram is Thunder, the colors which best complement your internal energy are in the green range, which are the expressions of Wood energy. But be careful with yellows, browns, and metallic colors. This gives you a basic framework for your wardrobe, using the recommended colors for your main garments and the others for sparse decoration.

Similarly, each of the eight trigrams has certain numbers associated with it. Try to use locations, items, or vehicles that have a preponderance of your favourable numbers; try to avoid those with a preponderance of your unfavourable numbers.

The Chinese Zodiac

The 12 animals of the Chinese Zodiac are probably the best-known – and possibly the least understood – creations of the ancient art of the imperial astrologers.

It is relatively easy nowadays to pick up a small booklet about the animals which will give you a quick summary of your personality, telling you which other sorts of animal-types you should marry and which you should fear; and perhaps giving you a prediction of your fortune for the year ahead.

However, the animals are best understood as spiritual symbols representing inner qualities of your personality. They are not always evident on the surface of everyday life, but are nevertheless at work as hidden forces in each person's life. In that sense, the animals of the Zodiac can be immensely useful and will tell you far more about yourself and those around you than reducing the complexity of human personality to one or two catchphrases.

Using the animal portraits on the following pages, you could examine your underlying attitudes towards Feng Shui, for example, or towards looking for a new home or going for an interview. You may see yourself in a new light and change the way you study this book.

Predictions

The use of the animals dates back to the dynasty of the Han Emperors, who ruled for four centuries from 206BCE to 220CE. However, they are thought to have originated under the First Emperor, Qin Shi Huangdi, who reigned from 221–210BCE.

At that time, China was overwhelmingly agricultural, and the predictions of the court astrologers for the regulation of essential functions, such as sowing and harvesting, had to be communicated to farming communities who were neither numerate nor literate. Hence, they codified essential timings using a system of familiar animals.

The central purpose of the Zodiac was to foretell vital meteorological developments, which differed from year to year. The advice would range from predicting whether the coming year would be wet or dry, what to plant and at what time of the year, and when to harvest the crops. Based on this system, a modern Chinese almanac will still tell you the days on which there will be spring thunder, when earthworms will appear, when the flowers will begin to open, and on which days there will be rain.

To make such forecasts, the ancient imperial astrologers organized teams of observers to make painstaking notations based on the movements of stars in the night sky. These observations were matched with the findings of natural scientists examining the laws of nature.

They were seeking evidence of an order beneath the apparent unpredictability and chaos of daily events. As their divinations became more and more accurate, they started to include the world of human affairs. Thus, the principles of the Zodiac came to be applied to auspicious marriage dates, appropriate days for signing business contracts, and the best conditions for undertaking new projects.

Originally, the source of all such study and prediction was the exclusive preserve of the imperial court. That is no longer the case, but Chinese astrological prediction remains an arcane art and although the annual almanac is widely used throughout the Chinese-speaking world it is likely that only a tiny percentage of those who rely on it have studied its deep, underlying principles.

The cycle of the twelve animals

The cycle of the 12 animals runs in a strict sequence, beginning with the Year of the Rat and ending with the Year of the Pig. The start of each of these cycles is indicated by a small circle on the accompanying chart. Find your year of birth on the chart and then locate the description of the spiritual qualities associated with that animal on the pages that follow.

Since the Chinese Zodiac corresponds with the lunar year, you will need to pay attention to the actual dates given on this chart. The lunar year normally starts in January or February.

○ 1900	31 Jan–18 Feb	RAT
1901	19 Feb–7 Feb	OX
1902	8 Feb–28 Jan	TIGER
1903	29 Jan–15 Feb	RABBIT
1904	16 Feb–3 Feb	DRAGON
1905	4 Feb–24 Jan	SNAKE
1906	25 Jan–12 Feb	HORSE
1907	13 Feb–1 Feb	SHEEP
1908	2 Feb–21 Jan	MONKEY
1909	22 Jan–9 Feb	ROOSTER
1910	10 Feb–29 Jan	DOG
1911	30 Jan–17 Feb	PIG
○ 1912	18 Feb–5 Feb	RAT
1913	6 Feb–25 Jan	OX
1914	26 Jan–13 Feb	TIGER
1915	14 Feb–3 Feb	RABBIT
1916	4 Feb–22 Jan	DRAGON
1917	23 Jan–10 Feb	SNAKE
1918	11 Feb–31 Jan	HORSE
1919	1 Feb–19 Feb	SHEEP
1920	20 Feb–7 Feb	MONKEY
1921	8 Feb–27 Jan	ROOSTER
1922	28 Jan–15 Feb	DOG
1923	16 Feb–4 Feb	PIG
○ 1924	5 Feb–23 Jan	RAT
1925	24 Jan–12 Feb	OX
1926	13 Feb–1 Feb	TIGER
1927	2 Feb–22 Jan	RABBIT
1928	23 Jan–9 Feb	DRAGON
1929	10 Feb–29 Jan	SNAKE
1930	30 Jan–16 Feb	HORSE
1931	17 Feb–5 Feb	SHEEP
1932	6 Feb–25 Jan	MONKEY
1933	26 Jan–13 Feb	ROOSTER
1934	14 Feb–3 Feb	DOG
1935	4 Feb–23 Jan	PIG
○ 1936	24 Jan–10 Feb	RAT
1937	11 Feb–30 Jan	OX
1938	31 Jan–18 Feb	TIGER
1939	19 Feb–7 Feb	RABBIT
1940	8 Feb–26 Jan	DRAGON
1941	27 Jan–14 Feb	SNAKE

1942	15 Feb–4 Feb	HORSE
1943	5 Feb–24 Jan	SHEEP
1944	25 Jan–12 Feb	MONKEY
1945	13 Feb–1 Feb	ROOSTER
1946	2 Feb–21 Jan	DOG
1947	22 Jan–9 Feb	PIG
○ 1948	10 Feb–28 Jan	RAT
1949	29 Jan–16 Feb	OX
1950	17 Feb–5 Feb	TIGER
1951	6 Feb–26 Jan	RABBIT
1952	27 Jan–13 Feb	DRAGON
1953	14 Feb–2 Feb	SNAKE
1954	3 Feb–23 Jan	HORSE
1955	24 Jan–11 Feb	SHEEP
1956	12 Feb–30 Jan	MONKEY
1957	31 Jan–17 Feb	ROOSTER
1958	18 Feb–7 Feb	DOG
1959	8 Feb–27 Jan	PIG
○ 1960	28 Jan–14 Feb	RAT
1961	15 Feb–4 Feb	OX
1962	5 Feb–24 Jan	TIGER
1963	25 Jan–12 Feb	RABBIT
1964	13 Feb–1 Feb	DRAGON
1965	2 Feb–20 Jan	SNAKE
1966	21 Jan–8 Feb	HORSE
1967	9 Feb–29 Jan	SHEEP
1968	30 Jan–16 Feb	MONKEY
1969	17 Feb–5 Feb	ROOSTER
1970	6 Feb–26 Jan	DOG
1971	27 Jan–14 Feb	PIG
○ 1972	15 Feb–2 Feb	RAT
1973	3 Feb–22 Jan	OX
1974	23 Jan–10 Feb	TIGER
1975	11 Feb–30 Jan	RABBIT
1976	31 Jan–17 Feb	DRAGON
1977	18 Feb–6 Feb	SNAKE
1978	7 Feb–27 Jan	HORSE
1979	28 Jan–15 Feb	SHEEP
1980	16 Feb–4 Feb	MONKEY
1981	5 Feb–24 Jan	ROOSTER
1982	25 Jan–12 Feb	DOG
1983	13 Feb–1 Feb	PIG
○ 1984	2 Feb–19 Feb	RAT
1985	20 Feb–8 Feb	OX
1986	9 Feb–28 Jan	TIGER
1987	29 Jan–16 Feb	RABBIT
1988	17 Feb–5 Feb	DRAGON
1989	6 Feb–26 Jan	SNAKE
1990	27 Jan–14 Feb	HORSE
1991	15 Feb–3 Feb	SHEEP
1992	4 Feb–22 Jan	MONKEY
1993	23 Jan–9 Feb	ROOSTER
1994	10 Feb–30 Jan	DOG
1995	31 Jan–18 Feb	PIG
○ 1996	19 Feb–6 Feb	RAT
1997	7 Feb–27 Jan	OX
1998	28 Jan–15 Feb	TIGER
1999	16 Feb–4 Feb	RABBIT
2000	5 Feb–23 Jan	DRAGON
2001	24 Jan–11 Feb	SNAKE
2002	12 Feb–31 Jan	HORSE
2003	1 Feb–21 Jan	SHEEP

The Rat

Reaching out
*This earliest recorded
symbol of the Rat (left)
gives us the intuitive
impression of a little child
extending its arms as if
about to hug someone. The
Feng Shui character (right)
expresses that same
excitable, exploring energy.*

People born in the Year of the Rat often exhibit the distinctive characteristics that have made the rat family one of nature's most enduring species. The animals we know today as rats are thought to have existed on the planet long before the emergence of human beings and there is scientific speculation that they are particularly well suited to survive long after the human race has passed into oblivion.

In the Chinese Zodiac, Rats have remarkable qualities of persistence and endurance. Regardless of what happens to them and the varying conditions they encounter, they always seem to have the ability to adapt and carry on. Unlike those who complain if they face difficult circumstances or who are crushed by heavy pressure, Rats have the ability to accept whatever happens to them. Whether it manifests in their persistence, their willingness to try new things, or their ability to adjust to changing circumstances, bravery is one of the hallmarks of Rats.

Their natural curiosity makes Rats keen observers, born artists, and inventors. They take a great interest in other people, but they must be careful because they have a tendency to talk too freely. Their friends find this attractive, but others may become resentful, accusing them of gossiping and speaking behind people's backs. Luckily, Rats forgive others easily.

Like the energy of their little animal counterparts, they are capable of great speed – they might be good runners, like fast modes of transport, and perhaps be able to work and communicate with unusual speed and determination.

You will often find a Rat moving around: changing jobs, changing homes, travelling; they just don't seem to stay put. They have many interests and there is a richness about their lives: it may be their various hobbies, their accomplishments, or their wealth. Their love of life embraces their eagerness to take risks and embark on adventures. It does not matter if success can be guaranteed, the Rat is excited by new things, new places, and new people.

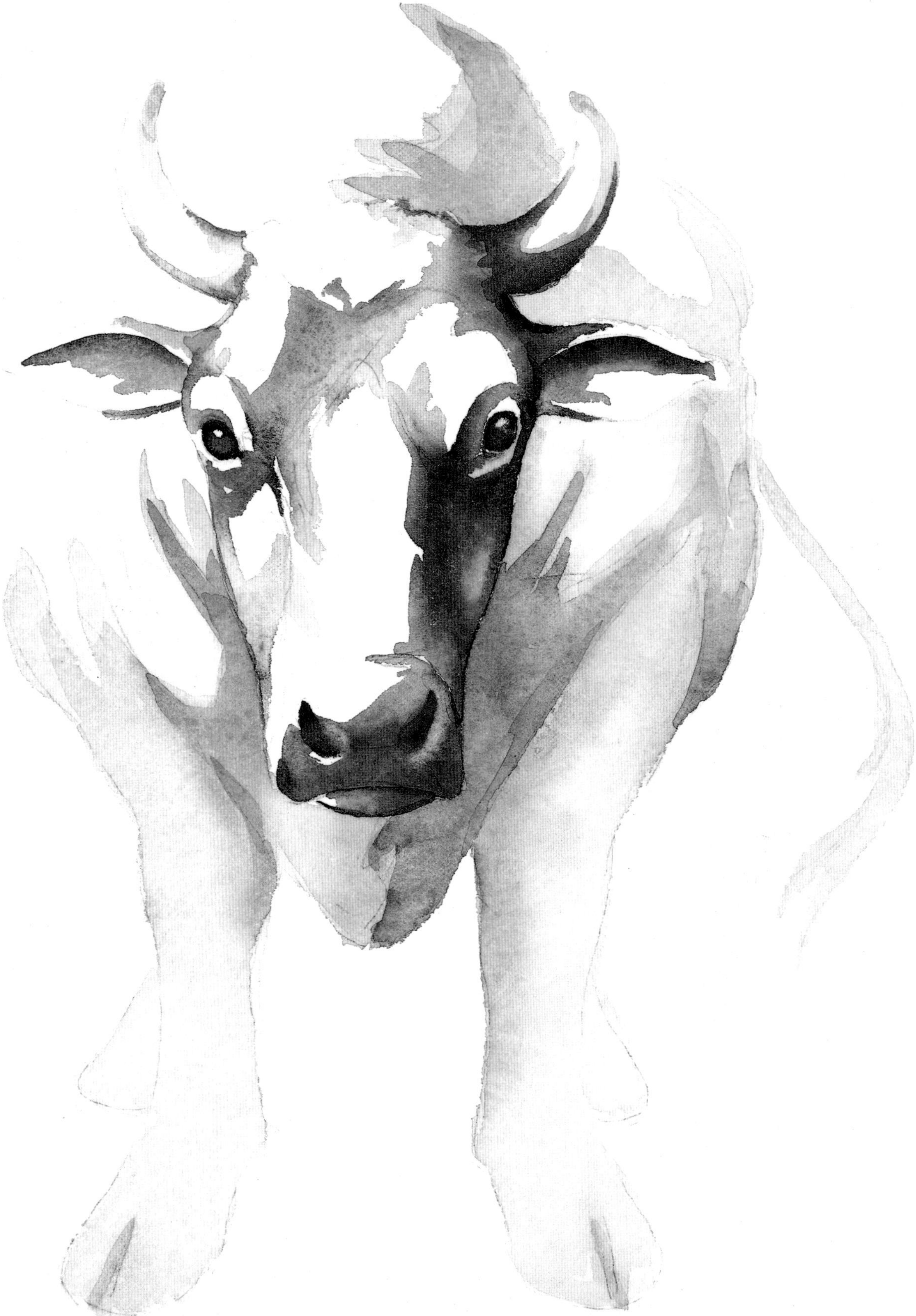

The Ox

Steady movement
This earliest recorded symbol of the Ox (left) is an impressionistic rendering with two horns, tail, and the power of a single rear leg which powers its steady forward movement. The Feng Shui character (right) captures the same sturdiness, a sense of power moving on the earth.

People born in the Year of the Ox are among the world's hardest workers, just like the oxen throughout Asia who labour in the fields and rice paddies, pulling the farmers' ploughs from early morning to dusk. Stamina and persistence is their great strength. They are not complainers and they can withstand considerable pressure. Not surprisingly, other people often turn to them for help and great burdens may fall on their shoulders. Their ability to carry those burdens is reminiscent of the heavy yokes placed on their necks which rest against the hump of the upper back.

Their consistency and strength make them persistent, even stubborn. Once they are set on a path, they are unlikely to deviate from it. It is hard for them to abandon even a course charted in error. In the same way, they are impassive. Even if they are beset with worries, and have strong feelings, they are likely to keep them to themselves and reveal little to the outside world. They are also likely to keep minor illnesses to themselves while giving others the impression that they are strong and well; when they finally admit to illness, it is usually a serious matter.

These people are normally found holding down the same job or remaining in the same profession or line of work for long periods – perhaps because they may need to work hard, without taking risks with their career, just to survive financially. They undertake whatever they are asked to do and make a sincere effort to complete it. They do not offer to take on extra work, but rarely do they refuse to help. They work quietly and seldom complain. They are reliable colleagues and noted for their honesty.

The Tiger

Full power
This earliest recorded symbol of the Tiger (left) looks almost like a bow, fully drawn, with its arrow already notched. Its power is fully present, waiting. That same strength is embodied in the Feng Shui character (right), evoking the tiger's broad shoulders and powerful haunches.

People born in the Year of the Tiger experience the full force of their primal energy with startling intensity. Just as with a tiger in its natural habitat, this immense energy field is in constant and intimate interaction with the environment around it. The power of the Tiger is deeply sensitive. It draws other energies to it. It is alert to minute changes, moods, and emotions. Once a reaction is triggered, the response of a Tiger's energy is breathtaking.

These people almost always give the impression that they are fully present. Even when resting, they are like a loaded weapon, lying gracefully at ease, but always primed. Their influence can be considerable, whether it be in relationships, in business, or in any other encounter: in China they are said to be like the steaming locomotive at the head of a long train. Often, their energy manifests in tremendous anger and, if that power is not disciplined, it can lead to frequent losses of

temper. A well-trained Tiger makes a ferocious fighter and a heroic soldier.

The natural power with which they are born brings them good fortune in life. When they are young they tend to do better than others in school and sports. They turn out to be natural leaders. This is due in part to the fact they are almost always ready to take chances. They often become spontaneous heroes, rescuing victims from accidents and disasters while others remain horrified bystanders. Tigers like to do jobs that give them a considerable measure of independence; if they have to be responsible to anyone, it should be the chief executive. But usually it is the Tigers themselves who end up at the top!

Their colleagues and opponents will often be wary of them, some may even be fearful. Their friends, lovers, and children relax in the knowledge that they are in the company of a powerful protector.

31

The Rabbit

On the alert
This earliest recorded symbol of the Rabbit (left) shows two perky ears raised like antennae on a creature who is looking straight ahead, fully alert, and ready to move on a split second's notice. The Feng Shui character (right) conveys the same sprightly energy that characterizes this remarkable creature.

People born in the Year of the Rabbit tend to be exceptionally sensitive and unusually alert. They exhibit a high degree of intelligence, combined with refreshing honesty. Their minds move with great speed. This enables them to complete a wide range of varied tasks in a surprisingly short time. Their speed and acumen is highly prized in the world of mathematics and accountancy.

Their cleverness also keeps them forever scanning the future, thinking ahead, detecting threats and risks. They always seem to have their eye on the nearest exit, and to have scouted out several simultaneous alternatives. This tendency can manifest itself in the ability of Rabbits to have several possible lifestyles up their sleeves: if one approach doesn't work, they are immediately ready with a substitute. They will keep on trying until they find a way out of any impasse.

These outwardly soft, sensitive creatures have a rich emotional life. Their feelings change as rapidly as unstable weather. They flick back and forth between happiness and sadness. Once seized with intense anger they seem to have little control over it, but that passes like a summer storm. The speed with which their feelings change, and their fast moving minds often leave them feeling impatient. Rabbits don't like to waste time and they are hard put to understand why everyone else isn't as quick-witted as they are. Others can get easily provoked by this, especially if they consider the Rabbit's impatience to be arrogant disdain.

Just like a small rabbit kept as a child's pet, the softness and vulnerability of Rabbits attracts us. They seem almost defenceless, both against a threatening world and also in the face of their own inner feelings. What seems to be supreme weakness can also be a remarkable gift. In any situation which requires acute awareness of the total environment and a lightning ability to compute alternative reactions and possible scenarios for response, there could be no greater asset in a team than a Rabbit.

The Dragon

Among the clouds
This earliest recorded symbol of the Dragon (left) comprises a swirling curve, like a masterful brush stoke, conveying the constantly changing character of the Dragon, coiling effortlessly in its spiritual abode among the clouds. The Feng Shui character (right) is a complex ideogram indicating that the Dragon can manifest its power everywhere – on land, water, and sky.

People born in the Year of the Dragon are endowed with a spirit of great power. For millennia, the Dragon has been the pre-eminent symbol in Chinese and other cultures of the Orient for the highest spiritual essence. It is the embodiment of wisdom, strength, and the energy of unending transformation. As the Dragon moves, it turns its head to see what has transpired as it passed by; it looks downward from a great height to survey the entire landscape over which it is passing.

The energy of the Dragon is the potential for effortless movement, the ability to undertake and accomplish vast endeavours, to think and work on a marvellous scale. Thus, with this energy, the person is ready to take up any challenge, to respond to any request, and to adapt to constant changes of plan. They are normally able to carry others with them, and to receive respect and support from those with whom they work, play, and live.

Dragons are at home in a world of dreams. They can detach themselves with ease from the inconvenient realities of daily life and direct their vision elsewhere. They are wonderfully creative. They make gifted artists and visionaries. In their fantasies, nothing is impossible. Yet despite their active imaginations, they are extraordinarily steady, firm of purpose, and solid. In fact, it can be quite a challenge trying to get a Dragon to change course if they see no need for it!

Their openness makes it easy for them to strike up a wide range of friendships. Sometimes their lofty attitudes and remarkable powers may make others jealous, but Dragons are not usually dragged down into such conflicts. They are blessed with good fortune, not merely because they enjoy good luck, but also because of their ability to adjust to the perpetual flow of life's changes.

The Snake

Two directions
This earliest recorded symbol of the Snake (left) expresses the power which the snake exhibits at both the head and tail of its fascinating structure, resulting in its mesmerising movements and the ability to rise vertically with its intent gaze. The Feng Shui character (right) also emphasizes these qualities with powerful strokes for both head and tail.

People born in the Year of the Snake are often endowed with highly developed qualities of sensitivity. As if they possessed the legendary intelligence of the snake family, these people frequently exhibit uncanny perception. They seem to be constantly alert. They have that rare ability to be able to enjoy life. When they find something that they like and want, they know how to appreciate it to the full. Whatever their goal, they will seek it until they find it or accomplish it.

This passionate quality is combined with the inner strength to stick with things, to see them through to completion, and to follow all the twists and turns of events with persistence. It is said in Chinese culture that if you decide to kill a snake, you should make sure that it is completely dead, otherwise it will recover its energies, sense your whereabouts even over long distances, follow you, and return the compliment! Timing is the speciality of such people. They are brilliant at lying in wait. They may wait months or years, patiently observing. Then, at exactly the right moment, they will focus all their accumulated energies and make their move.

It is best never to make an enemy of a Snake. But if you embark on a vast project which is fraught with difficulty, exceedingly complex, and of great importance, you could do no better than to have the Snake's wisdom and determination on your side.

Suppleness is the hallmark of all snakes and it is true of those born in the Year of the Snake. That is the secret of the powerful way in which they are able to use and concentrate their internal energy.

The Horse

Persistent strength
*This earliest recorded
symbol of the Horse (left)
resembles a spear. It is like
an arrow that has just been
loosed from the bow, or a
beater used for pounding
rice. It conveys the feeling of
a useful tool, strong and in
motion. The contemporary
Feng Shui symbol (right)
also conveys a sense of
powerful, natural energy.*

People born in the Year of the Horse often turn out to be the sort of people who are completely devoted to their work. It may be any task: raising a family, maintaining a home, running a small business, doing needlework, engaging in a hobby, or just getting on with the next chore. They are always willing to do the very best that they can and are genuinely devoted to the task in hand. Even if they are tired and face many obstacles, they are intent on completing the day's work.

This quality emerges from the strength and persistence of the Horse energy. It makes them great members of any workforce. Like the magnificent generations of horses that have carried human beings through all kinds of circumstance – on long journeys, into wars and across treacherous terrain – Horses display tremendous inner strength and determination.

They are not only strong, they are dependable. They are honest and loyal. If they make a promise, they do their very best to keep it. They will rarely let you down and they will hardly ever give up.

Even in the face of crises and difficulties, Horses have a tendency to go forward. They are always willing to summon up all their power for one last try. This tendency is also a sign of tremendous inner confidence. They are always ready to tackle the next level, to take on the next challenge. With the energy of a thoroughbred, they are eager to take the next jump or to cross the next stream.

Although Horses are proud, independent creatures, they need companionship. They need someone with whom they can live in harmony, to guide them and give them wise advice. Just as a good horse needs a rider and others to care for it, these people normally need a good friend or partner if they are to manifest their full power and spirit.

The Sheep

Steady under pressure
This earliest recorded symbol of the Sheep (left) resembles a body endowed with multiple arms and legs, or a useful rack, able to take considerable pressure and remain stable. The Feng Shui character (right) maintains the strong central line for the body, completed with the flick of a tail at the end of the brush stroke.

People born in the Year of the Sheep manifest a quality of energy which enables them to bear great pressure, yet remain stable. Just like the remarkable quality of the sheep who are capable of enduring extreme weather conditions and surviving on sparse vegetation, there is an unseen strength which enables them to survive changing circumstances. People with this energy may give the external impression of being soft, but they have considerable internal fortitude. This gives them the ability to survive even where others, who may appear more robust, cannot. Such people might be ideally suited to outdoor jobs, emergency relief work, and commando exercises where they work in small, skilled squads exposed to harsh environments.

Such people are extraordinarily hard workers, accomplishing not only their own assignments, but taking on the overload from others. Whether they are raising a large family, dealing with unfolding crises, doing punishing labour, or meeting impossible deadlines, they always seem willing to take on more. In fact, they neither like nor seek challenges, yet are willing to bear whatever is thrust upon them. Sometimes it can seem as if Sheep are people intent on working themselves to death. They will gladly offer to take all the pressure on their own shoulders and they seem to have the inner power to stick with something until they can barely move.

The steadfast quality of Sheep energy makes such people unusually reliable. They are rarely found in positions of great leadership. Indeed, when they have put in hours of hard, dedicated effort on a successful project, it is their managers who receive all the praise and the limelight. The Sheep remain in the background, without arrogance. They make excellent team workers and thrive in the company of other people. Like stately vessels moving forward with great determination, they are silent. They seldom complain. Their great strength is in their ability to listen, to observe, and to remain steady.

The Monkey

Quick as a flash
This earliest recorded symbol of the Monkey (left) is like the effort of a painter to evoke a flash of lightning with a single brush stroke. It has the feeling of the erect, perky monkey, alert and quick witted. The Feng Shui character (right) is filled with energy and skilfully depicts the Monkey's desire to emulate the human realm.

People born in the Year of the Monkey often have a inner spirit imbued with the lightning energy of our ancestral primates. Their minds normally move with remarkable speed. They have the mental gift of being able to learn quickly and, like all monkeys, to copy and imitate whatever attracts them. Their energetic intelligence also gives them the power to come up with new ideas, to invent new ways of doing things, and to dream up new systems and products.

The fast-moving energy of the Monkey person sometimes makes them appear insensitive to others. They get accused of being unfeeling, and their colleagues and friends may go through periods of being intensely irritated with them. Luckily, the nature of Monkey energy means that they come back again and again, are not easily angered, and are unlikely to bear long-term grudges. Although they are often highly independent types, these people are usually quick to make friends and can be extraordinarily helpful in times of need.

Normally, Monkeys find themselves born into families where they are well cared for. They have a great deal of self-confidence – even to the extent that they may think they are more accomplished than is the case. They are high achievers, constantly intent on self-improvement and have a secret ambition to be heroes. Their ambition is so great that they study hard in school, train hard in sports, are keen competitors, and are determined to win at whatever they turn their hand to. If they make an error they carefully examine what has happened, figure out what went wrong, and then carry on. They learn from their mistakes and rarely give up. In fact, their weakness may be not knowing when to stop!

The Rooster

The wine jug
This earliest recorded symbol of the Rooster (left) is close to the modern Chinese character for wine, resembling a container that can be used to contain and deliver whatever needs to be transported. The Feng Shui symbol (right) evokes a similar quality, but with even greater intensity of character.

People born in the Year of the Rooster tend to express their unique energy through the arts and human relationships. They are often extremely gifted musicians. They love singing, whether it be on the stage, at parties, or in the shower. Their creative spirit may emerge in other ways: in sculpture, drawing, painting, designing, or the performing arts. They have powerful imaginations and can be highly inventive. If their energy is not able to express itself artistically, it may manifest in scientific or commercial innovation or, more simply, in striking personal creativity, perhaps born of a rich fantasy life. They have the natural ability to focus their energy on what they are doing. When they are engaged in something they love, they put all their heart into it and they are capable of working with great speed.

Roosters have the strength of persistence. They exhibit considerable personal power. Normally, they know what they want and they make every effort to achieve it. These are not easy people to order around. They can be good talkers and are often the sort of people who

get used to winning arguments. They have an inner bravery, which makes them normally straightforward and honest in their dealings with others. They make wonderful friends and other people seek them out for advice and help with their own personal problems. Like their farmyard counterparts, they are watchful and alert to the changes taking place in the relationships around them.

The Roosters' temperament is like changeable weather. This can make them attractive to others, but it can also render them vulnerable. They may find themselves coming under the influence of others. They are often a little unsure of themselves and as a consequence may end up in situations where they are subject to the control of other people, whether at work or in their personal lives. When they have problems, they tend to struggle with them internally and may bottle things up for long periods. Rarely do Roosters fight back, but when they do, it is with an exceptional display of their full powers.

The Dog

Ready for action
This earliest recorded symbol of the Dog (left) makes us think of a weapon hanging on a hook, ready to be used, commanding respect, but not yet called into action. The Feng Shui character (right) rises up, like a dog sitting expectantly, ready to spring.

People born in the Year of the Dog almost always seem to be ready for action. Even when they are at rest, there is a sense of lazily coiled energy, like a spring that is ready to expand. This quality brings them considerable respect from those they know and work with. It is likely that they have already shown how brave they can be and have no need to be constantly proving themselves. Their bravery and prowess could be intensely physical, perhaps at a time of great danger. It could be mental or emotional, revealed in a willingness to enter into arguments or difficult situations fearlessly, often in a way that is clearly meant to help someone in difficulty.

Their inner power and their physical vigour makes them a great person to have on any team. They are loyal and reliable. They are normally found doing tasks that they like. Rarely do they run away from difficulties. Whatever they turn their attention to, they develop competence. They always find a way to complete their assignments. Because they have trust in themselves, are clear about what they are doing, and are devoted to the welfare of others, they have no need to call attention to themselves. They are wonderful listeners. In China, a person with that ability is said to have the soft ears of a dog! Their steadfast behaviour is born from the energy of that inner strength.

These people are graced with good fortune and deep feelings. They are appreciated and cared for by others. But, just like their canine counterparts, if no one wants to play with them, they are capable of amusing themselves on their own for long periods. They are not likely to be born leaders and are more often found to be excellent subordinates, carefully following orders. This can be a very fruitful relationship. If there is deep trust between leader and subordinate, both will be able to function to the best of their ability.

The Pig

Soft belly
This earliest recorded symbol of the Pig (left) emphasizes the softness and power of the large belly which is revealed as the pig sits up. This is an animal which is happy staying put. The Feng Shui character (right) evokes earth and sun, denoting the fact that the pig is active by day and asleep after dark.

People born in the Year of the Pig have a splendid quality about them. They are imbued with the energy of wealth. This may take the form of material riches, but it can manifest in many other ways. They are not obsessed by speed; they have a decent sense of time and are not hurried. They are not excessively worried about accumulating money; they may have modest means, but they are content with that. They are not driven by unreachable ambitions; they have their work to do and they simply get on with it. They are not panicked about getting ahead in life; they do not need to keep looking for new jobs or promotions. They are not intellectually competitive; they might even seem not so bright, but they are graced with natural humility.

Their energy grows and accumulates. This is often expressed in a rotund figure, even a little pot belly. In traditional Chinese culture, as in the figure of the Laughing Buddha, an expansive belly is a sign of great accumulation, whether it be of wealth, internal energy, content, or wisdom. The Pig accepts the richness it is given by life and has no need to demand more.

Sometimes mistaken for being sluggish, Pigs are highly intelligent, extremely perceptive, and have the ability to learn quickly. For all their weight, they can run quickly if needed. In times of difficulty, they become reflective, examining the situation and then proceeding with their solution.

These qualities combined together make Pigs unusually independent characters. They possess considerable determination. If they set their minds on anything they will pursue it with great dedication, even if, like their muddy counterparts at a feeding, they disturb others. That same inner power makes them great comrades, reliable and wise in times of crisis.

Your Feng Shui tools

In order to determine whether your own energy patterns are compatible with a particular property, you can use the set of distinctive Feng Shui tools which you will find on the following pages.

On pages 54–61 there is a set of eight circles. These correspond to the energy pattern in the property, depending on the direction in which energy enters it. On pages 68–83 there are eight octagonal "Ba Kua" (pronounced "baa guaa"). Each Ba Kua is a physical representation of the energy form denoted by the eight trigrams of the *I Ching*, as explained on pages 64–6. It corresponds to your own personal energy, according to your year of birth.

Each circle and Ba Kua is divided into eight interior sections, all converging on the center. Each of the interior sections is colored either red or grey. The red sections indicate directions which can be expected to attract, convey, or hold energies which are potentially beneficial; and the grey those which are possibly harmful – either within the property or in relation to the people who live in it.

You can therefore use these circles and Ba Kua to determine whether the inherent energy of the property and your own energy patterns are compatible.

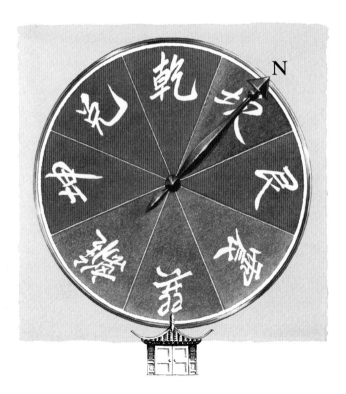

Left *Imagine the grey square is your home with your front door at the bottom. The direction you face as you enter the property is North West. Therefore, this is the Feng Shui circle for a North West house.*
Below *The Ba Kua for Heaven. Its arrow is also in the upper right corner. When this Ba Kua is placed over the circle so that the arrows are aligned, the red and grey sections match (see facing page).*

Using the tools

You need to start by determining the energetic pattern of the property itself. In Feng Shui this is known as finding the principal direction of the property. To do this you require an ordinary compass. Follow the instructions you are given on pages 52–3. Then follow the three steps below.

1. After you have found the principal direction of the property and the appropriate circle (pages 54–61), you will then need to select the Ba Kua which is relevant to your year of birth. You can do this by consulting the chart of years on pages 66–7.

2. Having identified the circle that corresponds to the direction of the property and the Ba Kua that corresponds to your year of birth, you should lay the Ba Kua on top the circle so that there is alignment between their centers and between the arrows for North. You can either cut out the circle and Ba Kua from the book or make a copy of the Ba Kua (using tracing paper), carefully marking the red and grey sections. The correspondence of the red and grey areas on the circle and the Ba Kua is the key to this exercise.

3. When you lay the Ba Kua over the circle, you will immediately see whether the red sections of the Ba Kua are aligned with the red sections of the circle. If those sections match, your energy is compatible with that of the property. If the red areas do not match, then your energy is not compatible.

Normally, among all the other considerations that a Feng Shui master takes into account, this would be one of the most important aspects that would be established when selecting a place to live. If you are moving home, you can use these tools to examine any of the properties you are considering. If the circle and the Ba Kua match, you will be spared many problems. If you examine your current home and the correspondence is unfavourable, you would be well advised to consult a Feng Shui expert for remedial advice.

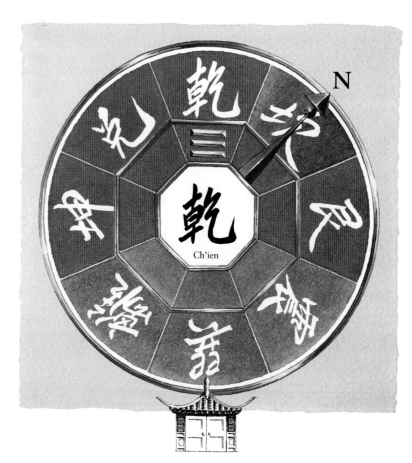

Choosing your circle

To use the direction-finding tools in this book, you need to know the "principal direction" of the property you are examining. This is the direction in which energy is moving when it enters the front door. It is therefore the direction which points away from the front door towards the inside of your house. Thus, if energy passing into your house, straight through your front door, heads towards the North East, your house is described as a "North East House".

Take your compass to your front door: in what direction do you move as you enter into the property through the door? This is the principal direction of your property.

Now turn to the next eight pages and select the Feng Shui Circle of that direction. For example, if the energy entering your home is moving towards the North East, you select the Feng Shui Circle entitled North East House.

NORTH EAST HOUSE

NORTH HOUSE

This is the Feng Shui Circle for a property whose principal direction is North,
as determined by the method explained on pages 52–3.

NORTH EAST HOUSE

*This is the Feng Shui Circle for a property whose principal direction is North East,
as determined by the method explained on pages 52–3.*

EAST HOUSE

*This is the Feng Shui Circle for a property whose principal direction is East,
as determined by the method explained on pages 52–3.*

SOUTH EAST HOUSE

*This is the Feng Shui Circle for a property whose principal direction is South East,
as determined by the method explained on pages 52–3.*

N

SOUTH HOUSE

*This is the Feng Shui Circle for a property whose principal direction is South,
as determined by the method explained on pages 52–3.*

SOUTH WEST HOUSE

This is the Feng Shui Circle for a property whose principal direction is South West, as determined by the method explained on pages 52–3.

N

WEST HOUSE

*This is the Feng Shui Circle for a property whose principal direction is West,
as determined by the method explained on pages 52–3.*

NORTH WEST HOUSE

*This is the Feng Shui Circle for a property whose principal direction is North West,
as determined by the method explained on pages 52–3.*

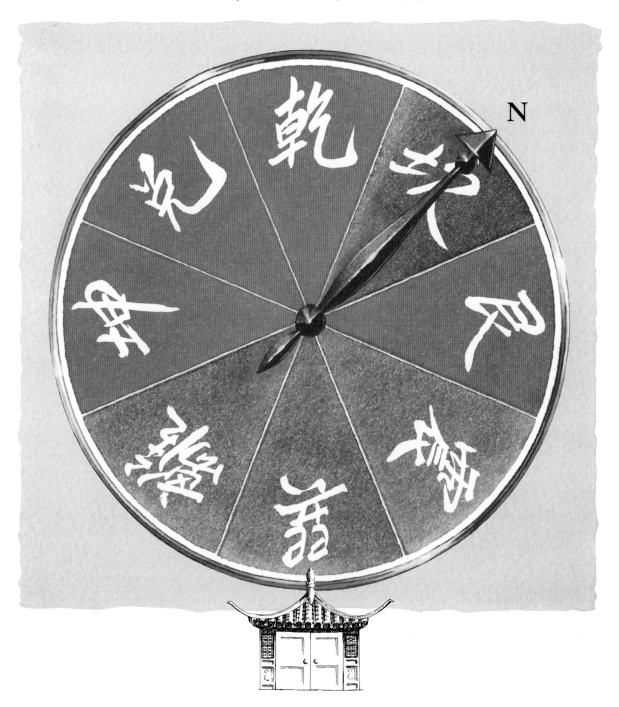

N

The Snake and the Monkey

This is a story of two very different people, born at different times and places. Each has a different sign in the Zodiac, a different trigram according to the *I Ching*, and different energy patterns in the system of The Five Energies.

Luke was born in Hawaii just as the Flower Power movement was starting to reach its peak in North America. It was June 1965, the Year of the Snake. His grandparents had emigrated from Shanghai to Hawaii in the 1930s, fleeing the warfare that wracked China throughout that period. Their three children were born in America and all had entered into mixed marriages. Luke's father had married a young woman who had moved from the West Coast to Hawaii at the beginning of the 1960s in search of a more peaceful lifestyle.

During his school days Luke was a first-class student and had a reputation for being hard-working and bright. He was always attracted to puzzles and his friends joked that he would make a great detective.

His fascination with seeking answers to difficult questions may certainly have influenced his career path. He developed a strong interest in journalism and, by the time he left university in the late 1980s, he was determined to become an investigative reporter. This decision was disturbing for his parents. It meant that Luke would likely need to leave Hawaii to seek employment with a major US news outlet. It was a highly competitive profession and one with many risks. He was still single and whether he would ever be able to settle down and have a harmonious family life was very much in question.

Luke's father had just taken early retirement and was not keen to be "losing one of his children" just when, for the first time in the life of the family, there would be more time to spend together.

He confessed his sadness to his own father, now in his eighties: "What shall I do, father? I feel I am losing my son, yet I have no right to hold him back from the future he wants."

The old man was silent and moved his thumb slowly over his fingers, counting to himself in the traditional Chinese manner. "This boy was born in the Year of the Snake. Am I right?"

"I think so. You know I never followed all that very closely."

"Snakes can only be stopped by killing them. If his heart is set, he will pursue his heart's desire no matter what you say. He will do well if he is given that freedom."

So Luke moved to the West Coast, stayed temporarily with distant relatives of his mother, and became a rookie reporter with a local TV station.

He was always inquisitive and intrigued by his own situation as the product of two cultures. From time to time, he would drop in to bookshops and browse through the growing range of books on oriental customs and culture. When it came time to find accommodation on his own, the thought crossed his mind to see if a book he had seen on Feng Shui had any useful advice. But it was simply too puzzling – even for him.

The next week was his grandfather's eighty-fifth birthday and he made a special point of calling long-distance to Hawaii. "Where are you living, Luke?" asked the old man.

"Oh, I'm moving out and looking for a new place," he replied.

"Hmm," murmured his grandfather. "Can you call me tomorrow? There is something I want to tell you."

"Why can't you tell me today, grandfather?" he asked impatiently – it was going to be a nuisance to have to call tomorrow when he would be out working.

"There is something I need to check."

Next day Luke called from a phone booth.

"Make sure the front door of your new home is facing North East or South West. And don't move in to a house with a door facing North, South, East, or South East," said his grandfather.

"That's a bit of a tall order, isn't it?" chuckled Luke.

"In *The Book of Changes*, you are a Mountain. You belong to the West Four. Do not go against your direction. You are a Snake. You have the power to wait for the right moment. Be patient. Avoid mistakes. You may have to make several turns to arrive at the correct destination."

Something in Luke stirred. Intuitively, he knew that his grandfather was deadly serious. Even though this impenetrable advice seemed to fly in the face of his desperate wish to find a place of his own, it was an instruction he would ignore at his own peril.

It took him a full eight months to find a location that corresponded with his grandfather's advice – and he sent him a hand-drawn map of the location, asking for his blessing. He got it, along with some advice about never having nine people to dinner.

Just about that time, a new face arrived at the TV station, a young French woman, Beatrice Dupont. She had been a primary school teacher in Marseilles, but left after a major disagreement with the local school board. She joined a public relations company and showed a real flair for new ideas and design concepts. But soon she decided to move into journalism, and successfully applied to work at Luke's station on a new team covering international cultural events.

"I'm looking for an apartment with a great view," she told Luke one day.

"When were you born?" he asked.

Beatrice could not have been more startled. "I was born in 1963. What's that got to do with it?" she snapped.

"I'll let you know tomorrow," said Luke.

He didn't bump into her again until the next week. "I got a place!" she said excitedly.

"Really?" said Luke, a bit taken aback. "Which way does it face?"

"Great view, large open balcony facing West, wonderful breezes all day…"

"Mmmm," said Luke, "I can just see my grandfather shaking his head…"

"What's your grandfather got to do with my apartment?"

"Well, he told me I should definitely have a home facing West, but it certainly wouldn't be good for you," said Luke. "Those West-facing windows of yours are going to be a real problem. You see, you're East Four and I'm West Four. I'm Snake and you're a Monkey. I'm Metal and you're Fire…"

She exploded: "I'm fed up with stereotyping. I left France to get away from precisely that." She turned to leave the studio.

"Good luck," said Luke quietly, "With those windows you're going to need it…"

Luke now heads a team of investigative reporters. Beatrice has left, frustrated because she could not express her creative spirit. From his grandfather's point of view, their varying fortunes can be traced to the fact that one respected basic Feng Shui principles and the other, perhaps because of her inherent qualities, did not.

The trigrams of the I Ching

The characteristics of change – and their resulting patterns – are analyzed in the *I Ching, The Book of Changes*, using deceptively simple combinations of three lines, known as trigrams. The combinations are made up of broken and unbroken lines. The broken lines represent the force of Yin, the female principle, and the unbroken lines symbolize the force of Yang, the male principle.

The trigrams are thought of as a family, starting with Heaven, the father, and ending with Earth, the Mother.

The trigram for Heaven, the father, consists of three solid lines, indicating maximum Yang power. The Chinese call it Ch'ien.

Then comes the trigram for Lake. A Yin line (broken in the middle) rests on top of two unbroken Yang lines. This is the youngest daughter in the family. The Chinese name is Tui.

After that is the middle daughter, Fire. The energy of a single Yin line emerges between two Yang lines. In Chinese, the trigram is called Li.

Next is the trigram for Thunder, known in Chinese as Chen. This is the eldest son. Two Yin lines on top and a single Yang line below convey the idea of energy arising.

Next in the family sequence is the eldest daughter, called in Chinese, Sun. This is the trigram for Wind. Here, the order of lines is the reverse of Thunder: the upward rising bottom line is Yin; the two on top are Yang.

Then comes the trigram for Water. This is the middle son. Here, the Yang power is in the central line, surrounded by two Yin lines. The Chinese name is Hum (K'an).

The youngest son is the last of the children.

This is the trigram for Mountain, called in Chinese, Ken. Two Yin lines are placed under a solid Yang line on top.

Finally, there is ultimate Yin, the mother. This is the trigram for Earth, represented by three Yin lines. The Chinese name is K'un.

The trinities of Yin and Yang lines that make up the eight trigrams represent all the fundamental conditions on Earth and in the cosmos. The eight trigrams also represent the eight directions and each also has its corresponding place in the cycles of the seasons and hours.

In this way, each person, according to their year of birth corresponds to a fundamental pattern of energy represented by one of the eight trigrams. That pattern can be displayed in the form of an eight-sided figure, known as a Ba Kua. This is a useful Feng Shui tool since it is possible to indicate within the octagon which of the eight possible directions are favourable for the person and which are unfavourable. This is clearly indicated in the eight Ba Kua on the following pages.

In addition to the general advice about the eight directions, for each Ba Kua there is a unique direction which is more auspicious than the others. This particular direction is given for each Ba Kua in the explanatory text which accompanies it. You can then use that information, for example to position your desk in your office (see pages 128–9).

There is also a direct correspondence between your Ba Kua and one of the energy patterns in the system of The Five Energies (see pages 10–11). This correspondence is also described in the explanatory text and you are told precisely which colors and numbers are most compatible with your energy pattern.

Fire

Wind

Earth

Thunder

Lake

Mountain

Heaven

Water

The years of the eight trigrams

Now that you have used your compass and one of the eight Feng Shui Circles on pages 54–61 to establish the principal direction of the property you are examining, you should proceed to compare those energetic properties with the essential qualities inherent in your own energy pattern.

You need to start with the chart of 103 years on this and the opposite page. Each year corresponds to one of the family of the eight trigrams of the *I Ching* (see pages 64–5). There are two columns of correspondences, one for women, one for men. The difference between the two is determined by the variations in the movement of internal energy in the mind/body of the female and the male.

Find your year of birth and select the corresponding octagonal Ba Kua on the pages that follow. Then, as explained on pages 50–1, cut out or make a copy of the Ba Kua that corresponds to your year of birth. Place it over the Feng Shui Circle for the property and examine the alignment of the red and grey segments. If they match, the inherent energies of that property will certainly be compatible with yours.

Female		*Male*
MOUNTAIN	**1900** *31 Jan–18 Feb*	WATER
HEAVEN	**1901** *19 Feb–7 Feb*	FIRE
LAKE	**1902** *8 Feb–28 Jan*	MOUNTAIN
MOUNTAIN	**1903** *29 Jan–15 Feb*	LAKE
FIRE	**1904** *16 Feb–3 Feb*	HEAVEN
WATER	**1905** *4 Feb–24 Jan*	EARTH
EARTH	**1906** *25 Jan–12 Feb*	WIND
THUNDER	**1907** *13 Feb–1 Feb*	THUNDER
WIND	**1908** *2 Feb–21 Jan*	EARTH
MOUNTAIN	**1909** *22 Jan–9 Feb*	WATER
HEAVEN	**1910** *10 Feb–29 Jan*	FIRE
LAKE	**1911** *30 Jan–17 Feb*	MOUNTAIN
MOUNTAIN	**1912** *18 Feb–5 Feb*	LAKE
FIRE	**1913** *6 Feb–25 Jan*	HEAVEN
WATER	**1914** *26 Jan–13 Feb*	EARTH
EARTH	**1915** *14 Feb–3 Feb*	WIND
THUNDER	**1916** *4 Feb–22 Jan*	THUNDER
WIND	**1917** *23 Jan–10 Feb*	EARTH
MOUNTAIN	**1918** *11 Feb–31 Jan*	WATER
HEAVEN	**1919** *1 Feb–19 Feb*	FIRE
LAKE	**1920** *20 Feb–7 Feb*	MOUNTAIN

Female		*Male*
MOUNTAIN	**1921** *8 Feb–27 Jan*	LAKE
FIRE	**1922** *28 Jan–15 Feb*	HEAVEN
WATER	**1923** *16 Feb–4 Feb*	EARTH
EARTH	**1924** *5 Feb–23 Jan*	WIND
THUNDER	**1925** *24 Jan–12 Feb*	THUNDER
WIND	**1926** *13 Feb–1 Feb*	EARTH
MOUNTAIN	**1927** *2 Feb–22 Jan*	WATER
HEAVEN	**1928** *23 Jan–9 Feb*	FIRE
LAKE	**1929** *10 Feb–29 Jan*	MOUNTAIN
MOUNTAIN	**1930** *30 Jan–16 Feb*	LAKE
FIRE	**1931** *17 Feb–5 Feb*	HEAVEN
WATER	**1932** *6 Feb–25 Jan*	EARTH
EARTH	**1933** *26 Jan–13 Feb*	WIND
THUNDER	**1934** *14 Feb–3 Feb*	THUNDER
WIND	**1935** *4 Feb–23 Jan*	EARTH
MOUNTAIN	**1936** *24 Jan–10 Feb*	WATER
HEAVEN	**1937** *11 Feb–30 Jan*	FIRE
LAKE	**1938** *31 Jan–18 Feb*	MOUNTAIN
MOUNTAIN	**1939** *19 Feb–7 Feb*	LAKE
FIRE	**1940** *8 Feb–26 Jan*	HEAVEN
WATER	**1941** *27 Jan–14 Feb*	EARTH

Female		Male	Female		Male	Female		Male
EARTH	**1942** 15 Feb–4 Feb	WIND	MOUNTAIN	**1963** 25 Jan–12 Feb	WATER	MOUNTAIN	**1984** 2 Feb–19 Feb	LAKE
THUNDER	**1943** 5 Feb–24 Jan	THUNDER	HEAVEN	**1964** 13 Feb–1 Feb	FIRE	FIRE	**1985** 20 Feb–8 Feb	HEAVEN
WIND	**1944** 25 Jan–12 Feb	EARTH	LAKE	**1965** 2 Feb–20 Jan	MOUNTAIN	WATER	**1986** 9 Feb–28 Jan	MOUNTAIN
MOUNTAIN	**1945** 13 Feb–1 Feb	WATER	MOUNTAIN	**1966** 21 Jan–8 Feb	LAKE	EARTH	**1987** 29 Jan–16 Feb	WIND
HEAVEN	**1946** 2 Feb–21 Jan	FIRE	FIRE	**1967** 9 Feb–29 Jan	HEAVEN	THUNDER	**1988** 17 Feb–5 Feb	THUNDER
LAKE	**1947** 22 Jan–9 Feb	MOUNTAIN	WATER	**1968** 30 Jan–16 Feb	EARTH	WIND	**1989** 6 Feb–26 Jan	EARTH
MOUNTAIN	**1948** 10 Feb–28 Jan	LAKE	EARTH	**1969** 17 Feb–5 Feb	WIND	MOUNTAIN	**1990** 27 Jan–14 Feb	WATER
FIRE	**1949** 29 Jan–16 Feb	HEAVEN	THUNDER	**1970** 6 Feb–26 Jan	THUNDER	HEAVEN	**1991** 15 Feb–3 Feb	FIRE
WATER	**1950** 17 Feb–5 Feb	EARTH	WIND	**1971** 27 Jan–14 Feb	EARTH	LAKE	**1992** 4 Feb–22 Jan	MOUNTAIN
EARTH	**1951** 6 Feb–26 Jan	WIND	MOUNTAIN	**1972** 15 Feb–2 Feb	WATER	MOUNTAIN	**1993** 23 Jan–9 Feb	LAKE
THUNDER	**1952** 27 Jan–13 Feb	THUNDER	HEAVEN	**1973** 3 Feb–22 Jan	FIRE	FIRE	**1994** 10 Feb–30 Jan	HEAVEN
WIND	**1953** 14 Feb–2 Feb	EARTH	LAKE	**1974** 23 Jan–10 Feb	MOUNTAIN	WATER	**1995** 31 Jan–18 Feb	EARTH
MOUNTAIN	**1954** 3 Feb–23 Jan	WATER	MOUNTAIN	**1975** 11 Feb–30 Jan	LAKE	EARTH	**1996** 19 Feb–6 Feb	WIND
HEAVEN	**1955** 24 Jan–11 Feb	FIRE	FIRE	**1976** 31 Jan–17 Feb	HEAVEN	THUNDER	**1997** 7 Feb–27 Jan	THUNDER
LAKE	**1956** 12 Feb–30 Jan	MOUNTAIN	WATER	**1977** 18 Feb–6 Feb	EARTH	WIND	**1998** 28 Jan–15 Feb	EARTH
MOUNTAIN	**1957** 31 Jan–17 Feb	LAKE	EARTH	**1978** 7 Feb–27 Jan	WIND	MOUNTAIN	**1999** 16 Feb–4 Feb	WATER
FIRE	**1958** 18 Feb–7 Feb	HEAVEN	THUNDER	**1979** 28 Jan–15 Feb	THUNDER	HEAVEN	**2000** 5 Feb–23 Jan	FIRE
WATER	**1959** 8 Feb–27 Jan	EARTH	WIND	**1980** 16 Feb–4 Feb	EARTH	LAKE	**2001** 24 Jan–11 Feb	MOUNTAIN
EARTH	**1960** 28 Jan–14 Feb	WIND	MOUNTAIN	**1981** 5 Feb–24 Jan	WATER	MOUNTAIN	**2002** 12 Feb–31 Jan	LAKE
THUNDER	**1961** 15 Feb–4 Feb	THUNDER	HEAVEN	**1982** 25 Jan–12 Feb	FIRE	FIRE	**2003** 1 Feb–21 Jan	HEAVEN
WIND	**1962** 5 Feb–24 Jan	EARTH	LAKE	**1983** 13 Feb–1 Feb	MOUNTAIN			

HEAVEN

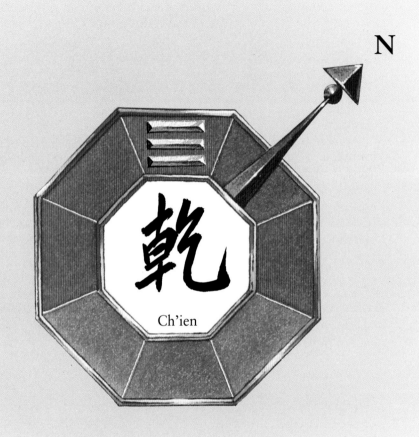

Ch'ien

N

Place this Ba Kua, which corresponds to your year of birth (see pages 66–7), over the Feng Shui Circle that corresponds to the principal direction of the property you are examining (see pages 52–61) so that the arrows are aligned.

Heaven

Heaven's energy is the maximum power of Yang. This is the creative and dynamic aspect of the life force when it is at its height throughout the natural world. In the human being it is reflected in inspiring leadership and the ability to carry a project through to its fruition. In the family of the eight trigrams, this energy is symbolized in the person of the Father.

In the system of The Five Energies, your energy is that of Metal.

Your Ba Kua is on the facing page. It belongs to the group known as West Four, whose energies arise in the West, South West, North West, and North East. Your energy will be complementary to any of the four Feng Shui Circles from that group. You will be able to see this immediately when you lay your Ba Kua over the circle that corresponds to the direction of the property you are examining.

Favourable energy comes to you from the West and the North West. But you may also benefit from energy that arises in the North East and the South West. You should be cautious about energy which comes to you from the North, South, East, and South East.

The colors which best complement your internal energy are golden tones, light greys, whites, and anything which is of a metallic or shiny quality since all these colors are the expressions of Metal energy. You will find the earth tones of yellows and browns supportive, because Earth is the parent of Metal. On the other hand, wearing predominantly bright fiery reds may tend to diminish your energy since Fire attacks Metal; too much green may have a similar effect since Wood energy tends to conflict with Metal.

Your most auspicious numbers are 6 and 7. Next in line are 8 and 2. A Feng Shui master would likely advise you to avoid the numbers 1, 3, 4, and 9.

LAKE

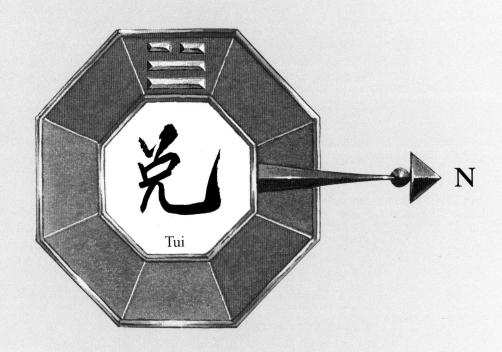

Tui

Place this Ba Kua, which corresponds to your year of birth (see pages 66–7), over the Feng Shui Circle that corresponds to the principal direction of the property you are examining (see pages 52–61) so that the arrows are aligned.

Lake

The energy of Lake is very fresh, with the quality of being alert and attractive. It conveys a sense of open-heartedness. This is the power of communication and being receptive to pleasure. In the trigram itself, a single broken Yin line rests on two solid Yang lines, as a new child is welcomed and cared for by its parents and siblings. In the family of the eight trigrams, this energy is symbolized in the person of the Youngest Daughter.

In the system of The Five Energies, your energy is that of Metal.

Your Ba Kua is on the facing page. It belongs to the group known as West Four, whose energies arise in the West, South West, North West, and North East. Your energy will be complementary to any of the four Feng Shui Circles from that group. You will be able to see this immediately when you lay your Ba Kua over the circle that corresponds to the direction of the property you are examining.

The most favourable energy comes to you from the West and the North West. But you may also benefit from energy that arises in the North East and the South West. You should be cautious about energy which comes to you from the North, South, East, and South East.

The colors which best complement your internal energy are gold, light grey, white, and anything which is of a metallic or shiny quality since all these colors are the expressions of the Metal energy. You will find the earth tones of yellows and browns supportive, since Earth is the parent of Metal. On the other hand, bright fiery reds may tend to sap your energy since Fire attacks Metal; greens may have a similar effect since Wood energy tends to conflict with Metal.

Your most auspicious numbers are 6 and 7. Next in line are 8 and 2. A Feng Shui master would likely advise you to avoid the numbers 1, 3, 4, and 9.

FIRE

Li

N

Place this Ba Kua, which corresponds to your year of birth (see pages 66–7), over the Feng Shui Circle that corresponds to the principal direction of the property you are examining (see pages 52–61) so that the arrows are aligned.

Fire

Fire energy is explosive. Its power is capable of driving two forces apart, just as in the trigram two strong Yang lines are pushed apart by the power of a single Yin line in the middle. This power exposes whatever is hidden. Its clarity and intelligence bring insight and illumination. In the family of the eight trigrams, this energy is symbolized in the person of the Middle Daughter.

In the system of The Five Energies, your energy is also that of Fire.

Your Ba Kua is on the facing page. It belongs to the group known as East Four, whose energies arise in the East, South East, North, and South. Your energy will be complementary to any of the four Feng Shui Circles from that group. You will be able to see this immediately when you lay your Ba Kua over the circle that corresponds to the direction of the property you are examining.

The most favourable energy comes to you from the South and the East, but you may also benefit from energy that arises in the South East and North. You should be cautious about energy which comes to you from the West, North West, South West, and North East.

The color which best complements your internal energy is the red of fire, but it should be complemented with a little green, since green (Wood) is the parent of red (Fire) and your Fire needs constant fuel. Just as water puts out fire in ordinary life, so, too, the wearing of dark blues, dark greys, and black will tone down your energy. Excessive use of these colors could depress your natural energy. Similarly, don't overdo the Metal colors of gold and silver, or metallic tones. These, too, will drain some of your energy, as metal drains heat when it melts.

Your most auspicious numbers are 3, 4, and 9. A Feng Shui master would probably advise you to avoid the numbers 1, 2, 6, 7, and 8.

THUNDER

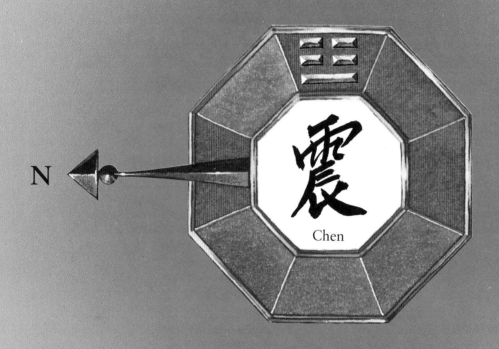

N

震

Chen

Place this Ba Kua, which corresponds to your year of birth (see pages 66–7), over the Feng Shui Circle that corresponds to the principal direction of the property you are examining (see pages 52–61) so that the arrows are aligned.

Thunder

Thunder's energy is like the sudden release of stored energy. Like thunder, it has the extraordinary power and speed of a spark born of the forces of Yin and Yang. In the trigram you can see the force of a single, powerful Yang line on the bottom driving upwards through the two broken Yin lines above it. But this power is not necessarily destructive. Like the power of all Nature's elements, it can give inexhaustible support to those who depend upon it. In the family of the eight trigrams, this energy is symbolized in the person of the Eldest Son.

In the system of The Five Energies, your energy is that of Wood.

Your Ba Kua is on the facing page. It belongs to the group known as East Four, whose energies arise in the East, South East, North, and South. Your energy will be complementary to any of the four Feng Shui Circles from that group. You will be able to see this immediately when you lay your Ba Kua over the circle that corresponds to the direction of the property you are examining.

The most favourable energy comes to you from the East and the South East. But you may also benefit from energy that arises in the North and the South. You should be cautious about energy which comes to you from the West, North West, South West, and North East.

The colors which best complement your internal energy are in the green range, which are the expressions of Wood energy. You could add in a bit of red, dark blue, black, and grey. Since Water is the parent of Wood, you will find dark blue shades or tones supportive. On the other hand, yellow and browns may tend to drain your energy since Wood controls Earth. Whites, silvers, golds, and metallic colors may have a similar effect since Metal energy tends to conflict with Wood.

Your most auspicious numbers are 3 and 4. Next in line are 9 and 1. A Feng Shui master would likely advise you to avoid the numbers 2, 6, 7, and 8.

WIND

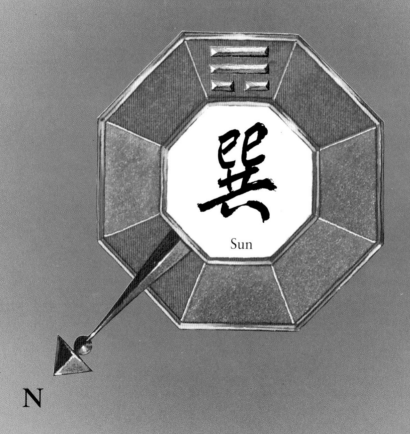

Sun

N

Place this Ba Kua, which corresponds to your year of birth (see pages 66–7), over the Feng Shui Circle that corresponds to the principal direction of the property you are examining (see pages 52–61) so that the arrows are aligned.

Wind

The energy of Wind is unseen yet irresistible. It is gentle, yet it persists. Like a breeze slowly shaping the rocks on mountain peaks, its patience and hard work overcomes whatever stands in its way. There is a generous quality to the energy: the quiet industry of Wind brings benefit to others, just as in the trigram the energy of the single broken Yin line moves upward towards the two solid Yang lines. In the family of the eight trigrams, this energy is symbolized in the person of the Eldest Daughter.

In the system of The Five Energies, your energy is that of Wood.

Your Ba Kua is on the facing page. It belongs to the group known as East Four, whose energies arise in the East, South East, North, and South. Your energy will be complementary to any of the four Feng Shui Circles from that group. You will be able to see this immediately when you lay your Ba Kua over the circle that corresponds to the direction of the property you are examining.

The most favourable energy comes to you from the South East and the East. But you may also benefit from energy that arises in the North and the South. You should be cautious about energy which comes to you from the West, North West, South West, and and North East.

The colors which best complement your internal energy are in the green range, which are the expressions of Wood energy. You could add in a bit of red, dark blue, black, and grey. Since Water is the parent of Wood, you will find dark blue shades or tones supportive. On the other hand, yellow and browns may tend to drain your energy since Wood controls Earth. Whites, silvers, golds, and metallic colors may have a similar effect since Metal energy tends to conflict with Wood.

Your most auspicious numbers are 3 and 4. Next in line are 9 and 1. A Feng Shui master would likely advise you to avoid the numbers 2, 6, 7, and 8.

WATER

Place this Ba Kua, which corresponds to your year of birth (see pages 66–7), over the Feng Shui Circle that corresponds to the principal direction of the property you are examining (see pages 52–61) so that the arrows are aligned.

Water

The energy of Water is mysterious. It moves downwards, just as water seeks the lowest level in nature. The power of this energy is deep, dark, and cold. There is great strength in its descent, for there is both withdrawal from that which surrounds it and unseen accumulation in its depths. Within this energy there is considerable uncertainty, danger, and great difficulty. In the trigram, the outer surface suggests softness in the form of the two broken Yin lines, yet they conceal a powerful, unbroken Yang line – just as water itself seems so soft and yet is more powerful than the hardest rock. In the family of the eight trigrams, this energy is symbolized in the person of the Middle Son.

In the system of The Five Energies, your energy is also that of Water.

Your Ba Kua is on the facing page. It belongs to the group known as East Four, whose energies arise in the East, South East, North, and South. Your energy will be complementary to any of the four Feng Shui Circles from that group. You will be able to see this immediately when you lay your Ba Kua over the circle that corresponds to the direction of the property you are examining.

The most favourable energy comes to you from the North and the South. But you may also benefit from energy that arises in the East and the South East. You should be cautious about energy which comes to you from the West, North West, South West, and and North East.

The colors which best complement your internal energy are deep blue and grey, which express Water energy. You could add in a bit of red or green to offset the darkness of the main colors. Since Metal is the parent of Water, you will find golds and silvers supportive. On the other hand, yellows and browns may tend to drain your energy since Earth acts as a barrier to Water. An excess of strong reds may have a similar effect since Water energy is opposed to Fire.

Your most auspicious numbers are 1 and 9. Next in line are 3 and 4. A Feng Shui master would likely advise you to avoid the numbers 2, 6, 7, and 8.

MOUNTAIN

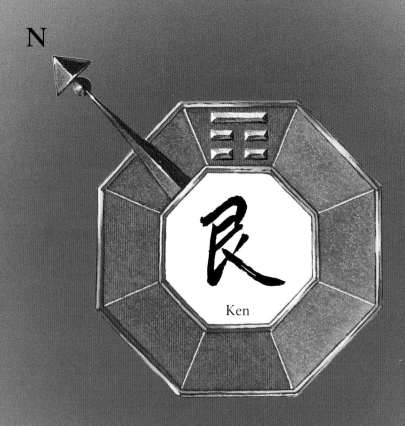

N

Ken

Place this Ba Kua, which corresponds to your year of birth (see pages 66–7), over the Feng Shui Circle that corresponds to the principal direction of the property you are examining (see pages 52–61) so that the arrows are aligned.

Mountain

The unshakeable power of Mountain's energy lies in its stillness. Like a great mountain, it is tranquil. Like a meditation master, this silent force is born of understanding and inner strength. It is not a private power: it is a source of regeneration and inspiration for all it touches. As in the trigram, the active Yang line on the surface derives its profound support from the double lines of Yin at the base. In the family of the eight trigrams, this energy is symbolized in the person of the Youngest Son.

In the system of The Five Energies, your energy is that of Earth.

Your Ba Kua is on the facing page. It belongs to the group known as West Four, whose energies arise in the West, South West, North West, and North East. Your energy will be complementary to any of the four Feng Shui Circles from that group. You will be able to see this immediately when you lay your Ba Kua over the circle that corresponds to the direction of the property you are examining.

The most favourable energy comes to you from the North East and the South West. But you may also benefit from energy that arises in the West and the North West. You should be cautious about energy which comes to you from the North, South, East, and South East.

The colors which best complement your internal energy are yellows and browns, which are the expressions of Earth energy. You will find red tones supportive, since Fire is the parent of Earth. On the other hand, greens may tend to diminish your energy since Wood controls Earth and blues may have a similar effect since Water energy tends to conflict with Earth.

Your most auspicious numbers are 2 and 8. Next in line are 6 and 7. A Feng Shui master would likely advise you to avoid the numbers 1, 3, 4, and 9.

EARTH

Place this Ba Kua, which corresponds to your year of birth (see pages 66–7), over
the Feng Shui Circle that corresponds to the principal direction of the property you
are examining (see pages 52–61) so that the arrows are aligned.

Earth

Earth is the nurturing energy of Yin at its fullest. It is the sustaining power of the planet which gives birth to and embraces all forms of life. It is fertile, accommodating, and tolerant. Out of it emerges unconditional acceptance and natural responsiveness. This is the power to give nourishment and be present under all circumstances. In the family of the eight trigrams, this energy is symbolized in the person of the Mother.

In the system of The Five Energies, your energy is also that of Earth.

Your Ba Kua is on the facing page. It belongs to the group known as West Four, whose energies arise in the West, South West, North West, and North East. Your energy will be complementary to any of the four Feng Shui Circles from that group. You will be able to see this immediately when you lay your Ba Kua over the circle that corresponds to the direction of the property you are examining.

The most favourable energy comes to you from the South West and the North East. But you may also benefit from energy that arises in the West and the North West. You should be cautious about energy which comes to you from the North, South, East, and South East.

The colors which best complement your internal energy are yellows and browns, which are the expressions of Earth energy. Since Fire is the parent of Earth, you will find red tones supportive. On the other hand, greens may tend to diminish your energy since Wood controls Earth; blues may have a similar effect since Water energy tends to conflict with Earth.

Your most auspicious numbers are 2 and 8. Next in line are 6 and 7. A Feng Shui master would likely advise you to avoid the numbers 1, 3, 4, and 9.

Figures in a garden, painted
in ink and colors on silk by
Wang Zhenpeng (14th
century).

The Harmonious Positions

The harmonious positions

Feng Shui is a detailed science with many different analytical tools. The same home or office can be studied from varying viewpoints, using different methods of investigation. In this book, you are provided with a range of tools and "mirrors" from the Feng Shui repertoire. Part Two introduces you to a further tool, the Feng Shui view finder (see pages 90–1). This book goes one step further than its best selling predecessor, *The Feng Shui Handbook*, by focusing on your particular needs and situation.

The Feng Shui practitioner does not start with the assumption that there is only one way of going about things. Nor is there a belief in the existence of a perfect solution to every problem. In the Feng Shui world view, we are constantly being affected by many influences and just as nothing is constant, so nothing is forever "right". Feng Shui also offers an immensely pragmatic approach to our circumstances: we may simply not be able to "fix" everything. If we find that our energy patterns are not compatible with the property where we live, we may not be able to afford the luxury of selling it and moving somewhere else. We may work in an office that contradicts all Feng Shui principles, but that doesn't mean we can convince the boss to tear down the walls and start again.

The order of priority
The solution to these apparently insoluble conflicts is an order of priority in which you should use the various Feng Shui tools (such as the circles and the Ba Kua, the Feng Shui view finder and the directions that correspond to your trigram). If you can't bring your location or your furniture into line with the principles of the first methodology, proceed to the next

one to see what changes you can make. Keep going until you have seen what is possible using all the methods you have to hand.

Begin with Part One of this book, where you learned to establish your essential qualities. First, identify your place in the Zodiac and understand that your inner spirit is your strength and not something you should seek to change. It will help shape the way you approach the whole subject of Feng Shui.

Then, you can use the eight circles and the eight Ba Kua to see if the place where you live is compatible with your own energy patterns – or you can use those tools to assess your compatibility with places you might be considering moving into. Remember that nothing in the world of Feng Shui is ever 100 percent perfect, so if your home turns out not to be compatible with you, don't despair. There are still other things you can do to improve your situation. If you are very nervous about examining your current home, then feel free simply to use this methodology to examine possible new homes in the future.

Move on to using the Feng Shui view finder presented in Part Two to examine the arrangements in your home and work place. There are many aspects you can look at and some you may be able to change. Each of those changes will be a definite improvement because they are centered directly around your own individual circumstances.

Using the Feng Shui view finder
"Where is the best place for me to be?" is the question that runs like a thread throughout Part Two. The Feng Shui view finder will help you find answers in a variety of circumstances. The view finder is a tool of the mind. It gives you a practical method of finding the most

harmonious location in a wide range of daily environments. You carry it with you in the way you perceive your surroundings and you can use it anywhere at any time.

You start using your view finder in one of the most basic ways imaginable – recognizing the subtle effects on your nervous system of different types of chairs. You are then shown how to apply that sensitivity to the arrangement of tables and other furniture in your home. The advice on Power seating (pages 94–5) shows how knowledge of your personal energy patterns (see Part One) helps you to choose compatible types and colors of furniture. You are then shown how to apply The Five Energies system to decorating your dining table for special occasions.

The idea is to create a composite model of essential Feng Shui techniques to help you work with the energy you encounter in ordinary situations. These examples give useful day-to-day advice, but may also stimulate you to think how the same principles can be applied in other areas of your life.

The principles of the view finder are then applied to sitting rooms, bedrooms, the kitchen, and bathroom. The domestic uses of this tool are completed with advice on gardens, greenhouses, and garages.

You are then taken on a Feng Shui tour of contemporary office environments. First, there is a demonstration of the circulation of energy inside offices, with corresponding advice about how to arrange furniture and people inside those spaces. Then, there is an analysis of the impact on human energy of today's high-tech electronic world with some advice about how to cope with the onslaught of the myriad vibrations that surround you. This is followed by various suggestions on how best to position yourself in various office settings and situations, including meetings, sales presentations, and interviews.

The rest of the book is devoted to the way in which Feng Shui principles can be applied in public places, such as restaurants, theatres and cinemas, and on public transport.

Part Two opens and closes with introductions to two further aspects of Feng Shui: numbers and crystals. Although space does not permit a lengthy description of Chinese numerology and the use of crystal or jade energy, you will find basic suggestions that you can combine with the rest of the advice in this book.

Making the best of situations
If you find that you cannot do things like change the position of your chair or your office desk in accordance with your personal view finder, then you may be able to make changes in accordance with your most favourable direction which is given to you in Part One as part of the explanation of your Ba Kua. This is explained on pages 128–9.

Throughout this process, the information on numbers and colors from The Five Energies system always applies. At the very least, even if you find yourself in a situation where you can do nothing but try to wear clothes in colors that support your internal energy, then you know that you are making the best of a very difficult situation.

At the same time, armed with a profound understanding of Yin and Yang, you know that the principles of perpetual interchange mean that whatever is dark now will inevitably emerge into light in the future.

Solar powers

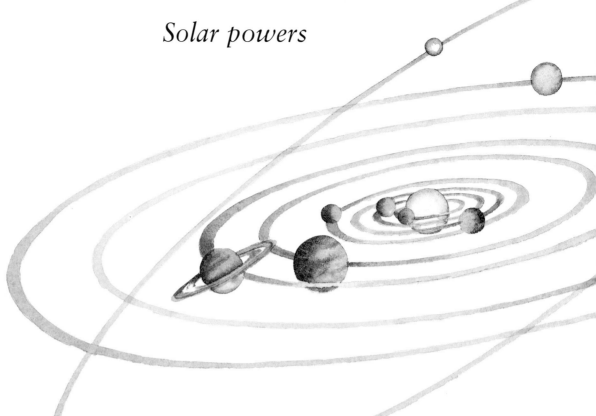

As the earliest natural scientists and astrologers of Chinese civilization contemplated the position of the human being in the universe, much of their attention was drawn to the energy which affected the Earth from the rest of our solar system. One very obvious example of this was the impact of the moon on the vast bodies of water covering most of the Earth's surface.

This attempt to understand the effect of our immediate surroundings in the cosmos was known as Ham, "looking into the heavens" (see pages 6–7). The insights of these early scholars revealed different patterns of energy striking the planet at different times and angles, and then dispersing over the Earth's surface in various directions.

These movements of energy also appeared to conform to certain cycles, so that the way in which the energy affected the Earth and its inhabitants changed every two hours, each day, every nine days, each month, each year and every 20 years.

Nine different energy patterns, or solar powers, were detected and each was assigned a number from 1 to 9. The study of these patterns and their relationship to the unfolding of human lives formed the basis of Chinese numerology. Each of the numbered energy patterns also had a correspondence within the system of The Five Energies (see pages 10–11) and the eight directions associated with the trigrams of the *I Ching* (see pages 64–5).

The number one corresponds to Water energy, the North, and the trigram Water. This energy is in constant motion and affects the harmony of our relationships with members of the opposite sex.

The number two corresponds to Earth energy, the South West, and the trigram Earth.

movement of all types, such as travel or changes of jobs and homes.

The number seven corresponds to Metal energy, the West, and the trigram Lake. This pattern is often known as "sharp energy"; it can either increase a person's power in certain types of conflict or may bring about harm, such as an apparent accident with a domestic knife.

The number eight corresponds to Earth energy, the North East, and the trigram Mountain. This energy is particularly associated with good fortune and the aspects of human life concerned with wealth, commerce, and finance.

The number nine corresponds to Fire energy, the South, and the trigram Fire. Like fire itself, this energy can bring warmth and happiness, particularly in our relationships; but if it is too intense it can generate destructive outbursts.

This energy affects the health of the body and is often associated with very common conditions, such as food poisoning or fevers.

The number three corresponds to Wood energy, the East, and the trigram Thunder. This energy is often associated with conflicts of all types, ranging from ordinary arguments to legal battles.

The number four corresponds to Wood energy, the South East, and the trigram Wind. This energy tends to affect people's futures and is carefully considered by Feng Shui practitioners when their clients are facing job interviews, exams, or situations that could affect their future reputation.

The number five is at the center (see the Lo Shu on this page) and therefore does not have the same types of correspondences as the other numbers. Being at the center, it is an extremely powerful form of energy, often likened to the power of a supreme ruler. If disturbed, it can affect virtually every aspect of a person's wellbeing.

The number six corresponds to Metal energy, the North West, and the trigram Heaven. This energy is associated with

4	9	2
3	5	7
8	1	6

The Lo Shu, sometimes known as the magic number box of Chinese numerology. Each of the numbers represents a different pattern of energy within our solar system. Their overall harmony is reflected in the fact that the numbers added in any direction always come to the same total.

Your Feng Shui view finder

Regardless of where you are, you can use the "view finder" on the facing page to help you understand the forces around you in any location. Based on an Ancient Chinese model known as the Five Animals – tortoise, phoenix, tiger, dragon, and snake – it can be applied in a number of different ways. Here, you will learn how to use it as a personal tool, to be applied to almost any situation in which you find yourself.

To understand how your view finder works, look carefully at the drawing. Start from the center and work outwards. At its very heart is a human being. This is you. When you look straight ahead, you are facing forward. This is the direction of the arrow on the view finder. Do not confuse the direction of the arrow with a point on the magnetic compass; this view finder works on a different set of principles to the house circles and the Ba Kua in Part One.

Surrounding you are four circles, each of which contains the presentation of an animal. At your back is a tortoise. In front of you is a phoenix. To your right is a tiger. To your left, a dragon.

Each animal belongs to one of The Five Energies (see pages 10–11) and the little white arrows show the movement of energy associated with them. Thus, the tortoise is dark blue for Water; its white arrows show energy descending. The phoenix is red for Fire; its energy rises up. The tiger has a white face, for Metal; its energy condenses. The dragon is green for Wood; its energy expands outwards.

You can understand the significance of these four animals by interpreting them from a psychological point of view, always imagining that they are placed around you in exactly the same positions that they are on your Feng Shui view finder.

Your nervous system is always aware that your visual field excludes movements and objects behind you. That is where you are most vulnerable. So at your back you want security and freedom from fear. This is where you want the strong shell of the tortoise.

On the other hand, when you look forward you want a clear, unobstructed view and you feel inspired when you are able to see a broad panorama. This is where the mythical phoenix flies. It is a bird of perpetual inspiration and you want that feeling stretching as far ahead of you as possible.

To your right is the place of the tiger. This animal possesses great strength, but it also has the capacity for unrestrained violence. Thus, the energy on that side must be carefully controlled (regardless of whether we are right handed or left handed) and that means having the energies and objects on our right relatively close to the ground, like a tamed wild cat.

To your left, coiling lazily above the earth, is the dragon. It is far-sighted and wise, but also stable – symbolizing our inner desire to have a broad outlook on life and a calm, open mind. In the Feng Shui model, this is the side on which you are advised to place tall objects which rise above ordinary eye level.

These four qualities have their physical counterparts everywhere in the world of Feng Shui. On the pages that follow you will see how you can use this model in very practical ways: to assess the psychological impact of furniture; choose the best position in a room in which to sit, eat, sleep, or work; arrange your bed; and establish secure, positive locations from which to conduct meetings or enjoy yourself in social settings.

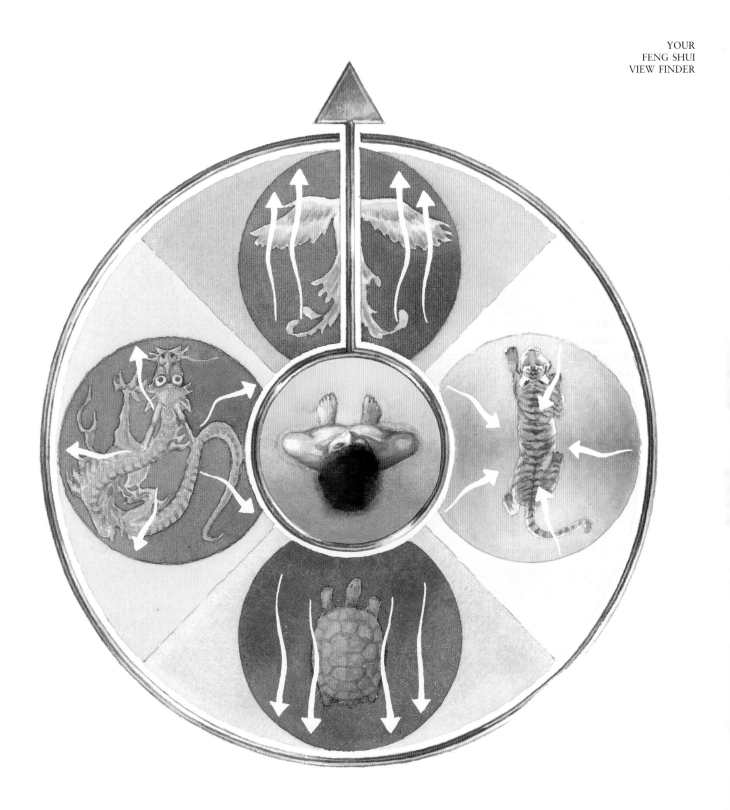

Missing animals

Here are four common situations in which you may find yourself. Each is characterized by one or more missing animals. Do you recognize the subtle feelings and disturbances caused by the missing animals?

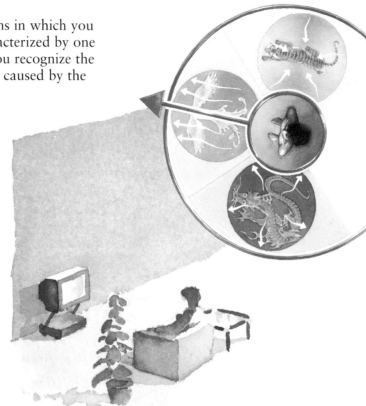

No tortoise
Many people find themselves sitting in the middle of a room with their backs exposed. They feel a slight breeze on the back of their neck, some awkwardness or unease. In the world of Feng Shui they are without a tortoise. Like this person sitting and watching television, their tiger, dragon, and phoenix are all correctly positioned, but the rear quadrant of their personal space is like an empty parking lot.

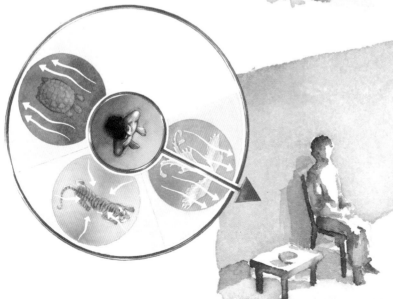

No dragon
A guard sits at one end of a long corridor. His chair is against the wall and has a good strong back. This secures the tortoise aspect. His forward vision is unobstructed and he has a clear view to either side: a wide phoenix aspect. The low table to his right fills up his tiger aspect and controls energy on that side. But he is without a dragon to his left, lacks inspiration, and may easily become bored and lethargic.

No tiger

The visitor, sitting in a large reception area, finds a chair against the wall near the corner and with a large palm to the left. This brings a considerable measure of security, complete with tortoise and dragon, and provides a wide open phoenix aspect. But the tiger is missing, leaving the visitor feeling slightly vulnerable.

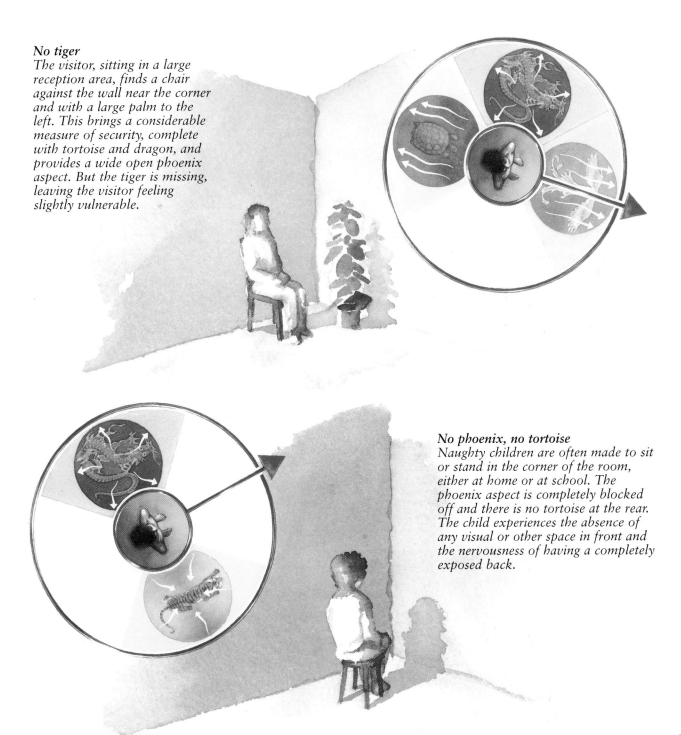

No phoenix, no tortoise

Naughty children are often made to sit or stand in the corner of the room, either at home or at school. The phoenix aspect is completely blocked off and there is no tortoise at the rear. The child experiences the absence of any visual or other space in front and the nervousness of having a completely exposed back.

Power seating

When you enter a room and are offered a choice
of seats, you can use your knowledge of The
Five Energies to find the best possible match
between you and the chairs or sofas. Choosing
the most harmonious configuration of these
subtle energies will keep you naturally alert and
create a positive energy field around you.

Wood
*This seat has typical Wood
characteristics. It is made from
timber and has an expansive,
elongated shape. The fabric is
green (the light spectrum for
Wood ranges from pale, yellowy
greens to very deep, dark forest
tones). If you are a Wood
energy person (the trigrams
Thunder, pages 74–5, and
Wind, pages 76–7), this is your
best choice. Since Wood
is the parent of Fire, a person
whose trigram is Fire (pages
72–3) will also find strong
energetic support here.*

Water
*This circular, dark blue armchair is definitely
the perfect seat for a Water person. Water
itself, of course, has no color, but the depths
of the sea contain and transmute all colors,
creating the unique vivid power of deep sea
blue. If your trigram is Water (pages 78–9),
your power will be all the greater in this
seat. As Water is the parent of Wood, people
whose trigrams are Thunder (pages 74–5)
and Wind (pages 76–7) will also find
support here.*

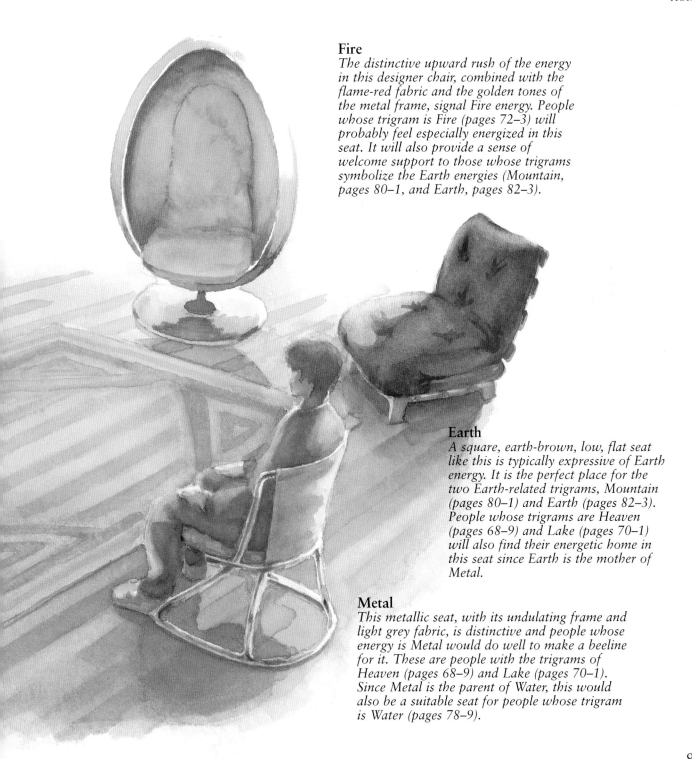

Fire

The distinctive upward rush of the energy in this designer chair, combined with the flame-red fabric and the golden tones of the metal frame, signal Fire energy. People whose trigram is Fire (pages 72–3) will probably feel especially energized in this seat. It will also provide a sense of welcome support to those whose trigrams symbolize the Earth energies (Mountain, pages 80–1, and Earth, pages 82–3).

Earth

A square, earth-brown, low, flat seat like this is typically expressive of Earth energy. It is the perfect place for the two Earth-related trigrams, Mountain (pages 80–1) and Earth (pages 82–3). People whose trigrams are Heaven (pages 68–9) and Lake (pages 70–1) will also find their energetic home in this seat since Earth is the mother of Metal.

Metal

This metallic seat, with its undulating frame and light grey fabric, is distinctive and people whose energy is Metal would do well to make a beeline for it. These are people with the trigrams of Heaven (pages 68–9) and Lake (pages 70–1). Since Metal is the parent of Water, this would also be a suitable seat for people whose trigram is Water (pages 78–9).

From stools to armchairs

When you choose a chair, you are choosing your base. The chair will be your camp, whether you are sitting down to eat, work, or watch television. It will be the platform from which you talk to visitors or literally "chair" a meeting. You should think of a chair as you would your home: it is the place that will give you support as long as you are occupying it. If it is weak or defective in any way, even as a temporary residence, the chair will not serve you well. In each of the examples below you can see the empty spaces left in the environment of each piece of furniture. Each may be used for a short visit or meeting, but it is by no means accidental that most people would prefer to have as their regular permanent seat a more solid chair, with all its animals fully present.

Only the phoenix
When you sit on a stool, whether it is a high bar stool or a low hassock, an old-fashioned stool with three legs, or one of contemporary design, you are exposed on all sides. This means that whichever way you turn, your phoenix aspect is assured. But it also means that you get no support from your tortoise, dragon, or tiger – all three are missing. Perching on a stool may suit you for a short period of time, but if you are going to be there longer, try to adjust yourself so that your back is against a wall and there are other people or pieces of furniture framing the space on either side.

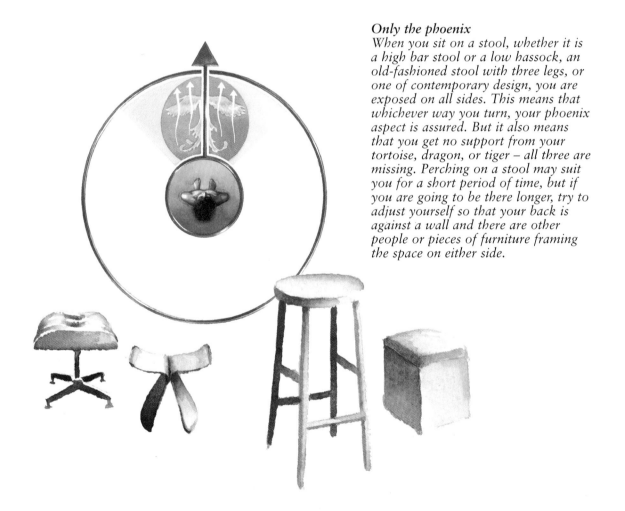

High-backed tortoises

These chairs have clear, open spaces for the phoenix, together with the advantage of powerful tortoise shells on the rear. But you do not have the full strength and security provided by a chair with arms. You are missing your dragon and tiger. We intuitively feel we are lacking something when we sit in chairs like these. On a deep subconscious level, we know that we would not feel comfortable or secure if we were to fall asleep. Our nervous system remains on guard.

All present

The power of these chairs derives from the presence of all four animals. We tend to feel much more secure in them and more relaxed. Physiologically, if we place our arms comfortably on the arm rests, the normal pressure which our upper arms exert on our torso is relieved. Our chest moves more freely and we breathe easier. Psychologically, we feel protected on three sides and able to direct our energy outwards. Our creative aspect is free to manifest itself. In Feng Shui this is represented by the phoenix flying ahead of us.

Table talk

Tables shape the flow of energy. Imagine that the six shapes below are stones that break through the surface of a stream of water. Imagine each one separately, surrounded by the running water of the stream. If you have spent time gazing at the patterns of water in a pond, by a river's edge or in a slow-moving woodland watercourse, you will be able to call to mind the way water flows around different shaped obstacles. This is how best to visualize the way tables shape the flow of energy.

Begin with the round table. The stream of energy smoothly divides around the circle and reforms, sending out calm ripples. When it passes the oval table, it glides effortlessly around one end, slides along the two sides and seamlessly closes up as it moves around the distant curved end. But when the stream hits the flat end of the squares and oblongs, a pattern of disturbed energy is set up and the angles cause shafts of energy to shoot outwards. In Feng Shui this is known as "sharp energy" and whenever possible, you should avoid sitting in the pathway of one of these angular energy bursts.

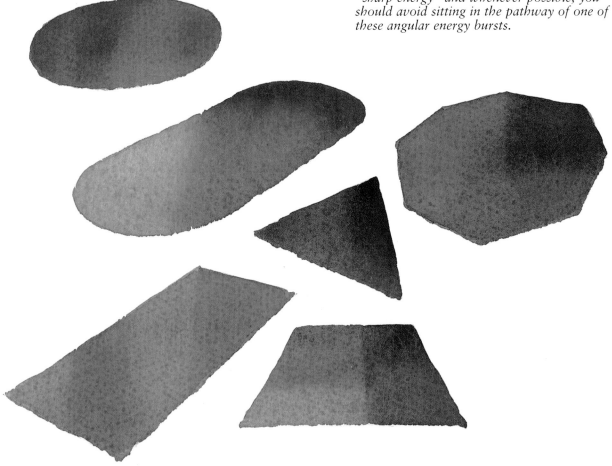

Wood and glass

A table is like a little earth, accepting and supporting whatever is placed on it. Wood and Earth energies are particularly suitable for tables. Wood energy controls Earth energy (pages 10–11) and helps keep it stable. Glass is made from sand, so it is part of the spectrum of Earth energy itself. Tables made entirely from wood or a combination of wood and glass conform to this principle, but metal is not as suitable (see below).

Hazards

Tables are meant to bear weight and provide a secure surface on which we can serve food, work, or place objects. If they do not have a secure base, they may be decorative, but they can prove to be a hazard.

Metal

In The Five Energies system, Metal energy can harm Wood if it is too strong, just as an axe cuts through a tree. And if Metal is too powerful it drains energy from Earth. Following this logic, metal tables are not recommended by Feng Shui experts.

99

Shapes and spaces

If you commit the view finder to memory, you can
apply it in any situation. For example, imagine that
you have come to the home of someone you don't
know well. You are waiting for them in a downstairs
sitting room. Which chair do you choose?

*This room offers you some good
choices. There will be no sharp energy
shooting off the round table. The
chairs and sofa have solid backs and
arms (although if the window were
open, the tortoise aspect of that chair
would be weakened). The seat the
person has chosen avoids the energy
flowing through the door or window.
Another good location would be the
armchair facing the window, but its
dragon and tiger sides are less
complete than the location on the sofa.*

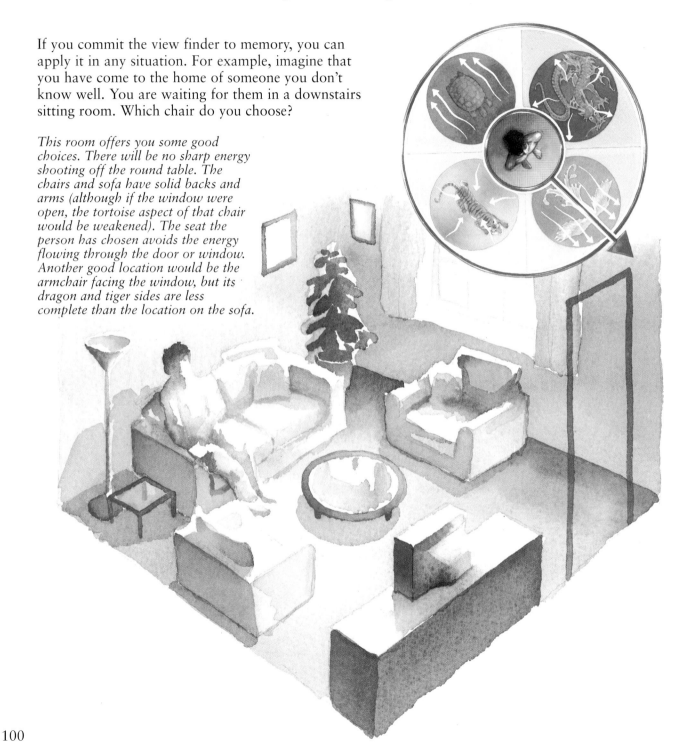

If you were asked to wait in this room, you might feel a bit unsure what to do. The seat where the person is sitting is directly opposite the door. The low table is on their left, but it should be on their right (the tiger side). The palm is on their right; it should be on their left (the dragon side). If you were to sit in the seat next to them, the sharp energy from the triangular table would shoot directly towards you. The low stool is likely to make you feel somewhat insecure; at the very least, you would want to move the stool towards the corner so your back was closer to the wall with the low table on your tiger side. You might prefer the chair opposite, in front of the window, making sure the window was closed or the curtain drawn to support your tortoise aspect.

101

Focal points

People often organize their sitting rooms around a central point. This need not be in the center of the room, but it is the area of the room around which most activity takes place. In many homes, the focal point of the sitting room is the television. The family whose front room is shown above has managed to arrange themselves so that they can watch the TV, but not violate fundamental Feng Shui principles. The TV is on a free-standing bookcase which has been positioned so that it acts as a barrier to energy entering through the door. The chairs facing the TV can then all be placed so that they have strong tortoise aspects and a good complement of dragons and tigers.

This family likes to sit around the fireplace. That is their focal point. However, you can see the problems this creates from a Feng Shui point of view, partly because of the position of the door. When the door is open, the energy entering the room disturbs the area immediately behind the sofa. The sofa, placed in the center of the room, is without a strong tortoise. Whoever sits in the chair to the left of the sofa is directly exposed to incoming energy disturbance from the door. Your view finder would most likely encourage you to sit in the chair furthest from the door because, although its dragon and tiger are reversed, it has the strongest tortoise and a reasonably clear phoenix aspect.

Sleepers

You can take your view finder with you to bed. You need a good night's sleep and you spend up to a third of your life in your bed. So it is important to ensure that the location of the area where you sleep is as harmonious, positive, and protective as possible. Use the fundamental principles of the view finder in exactly the same way as you would elsewhere in your house. You need a solid tortoise behind your head, a clear phoenix aspect ahead of you, and the proper config- uration on the dragon and tiger sides.

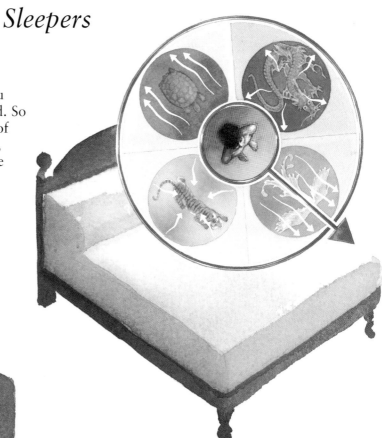

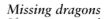

Missing dragons
If you were to sleep in either of these beds, you would have a strong tortoise behind your head and your phoenix aspect would be reasonably fine. But in both of these rooms, despite the different locations of the two beds, you would still end up with an empty dragon side. Your sleep would likely be a little restless.

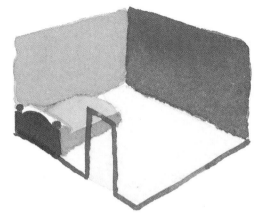

Missing tigers
When you look at the layout of these two bedrooms you can see that the position of each bed differs greatly, but the result is the same – in each of them you will be sleeping without a tiger. You would likely feel unprotected while asleep.

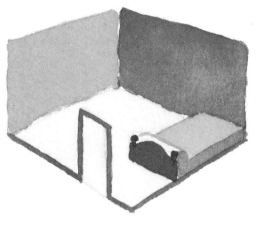

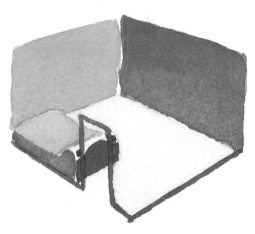

No phoenix
If you travel overnight in a sleeping compartment on a train, you can put up with having your bed closed off at both ends. But imagine sleeping night after night with the bottom end of your bed up against a wall or a large piece of furniture. Anyone sleeping in this position is sure to feel claustrophobic, since the phoenix aspect is completely closed off. The solution is to turn the bed around.

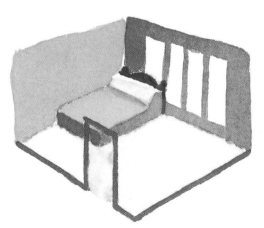

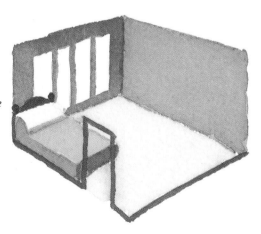

Weak shells
The significance of the symbolic use of a tortoise to describe the space behind you lies in the strength of the tortoise's shell, the extraordinarily strong house that it perpetually carries with it. Putting your bed with the headboard against a row of windows robs your shell of its strength, particularly if you open them.

The hearth in your home

No matter how high-tech your kitchen is, you are enacting an age-old ritual every time you cook. To the ancients, the hearth had great power, was often considered sacred, and was always respected as the place where the family prepared the sustenance that kept them alive. Therefore, in the Feng Shui world, the center of the kitchen is determined in a manner different to other aspects of the house – and this is regarded as so important that it overrides the use of your personal view finder. When you enter the world of the kitchen, you can leave your view finder behind.

The stove or cooker or hob on which you normally cook your meals is the central reference point in your kitchen, regardless of where it is placed. As this drawing shows, the back of the appliance is considered to be the tortoise aspect and the front end is the beginning of its phoenix aspect, which is where you stand when you are cooking.

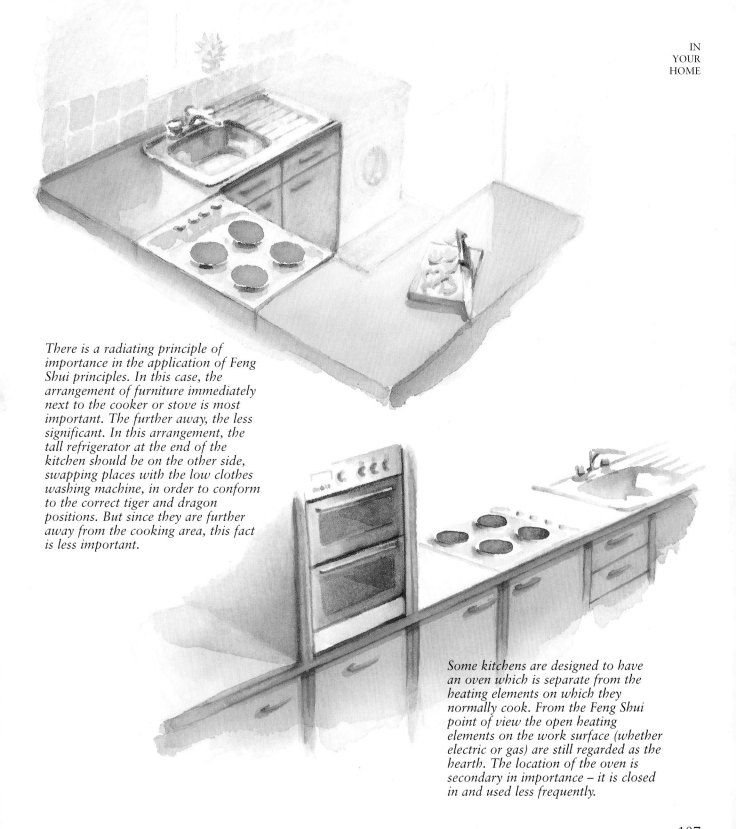

There is a radiating principle of importance in the application of Feng Shui principles. In this case, the arrangement of furniture immediately next to the cooker or stove is most important. The further away, the less significant. In this arrangement, the tall refrigerator at the end of the kitchen should be on the other side, swapping places with the low clothes washing machine, in order to conform to the correct tiger and dragon positions. But since they are further away from the cooking area, this fact is less important.

Some kitchens are designed to have an oven which is separate from the heating elements on which they normally cook. From the Feng Shui point of view the open heating elements on the work surface (whether electric or gas) are still regarded as the hearth. The location of the oven is secondary in importance – it is closed in and used less frequently.

Eating in

The family meal

It's a national holiday and you decide to have some of the family around for lunch. This time your husband is insistent: "We don't have to plan everything down to the last detail." But your instincts tell you that getting your family seated properly around the table is a way to make everyone feel welcome and respected.

Again, you rely on Feng Shui wisdom, especially since it comes from a culture in which family life plays a central role. You place your husband at the head of the table (1). You sit on his right (2). Your eldest son is on your husband's left (3). Next to you is your daughter (4). Opposite her is your younger son (5). Then you place your grandfather at the "second head" of the table, opposite your husband (6) with grandmother on his left (7), next to your daughter. That leaves a blank space, since your table can accommodate eight. In the Feng Shui world, you complete the circle by leaving that chair in place.

After hours

You invite your boss and her husband around for dinner. Altogether you will be six people with your husband and your two teenagers. Where should they sit at the table? Your husband is in favour of a casual approach, but you know from past experience that if you just let people seat themselves they can end up in some very awkward arrangements.

You want to be near your boss and you don't necessarily want her spending all the meal coping with the moods of your children.

So you decide to apply Feng Shui principles. Put your boss in a favourable location at the end of the table with a solid tortoise behind her (1). You should sit on her right hand and, if possible, have a good tortoise behind you as well (6). Put her husband on her left (2), near her but not in the most powerful position. Have your husband on your right side (5), a comfortable position, but further away from the guests. Let your two children occupy the remaining seats (3 & 4).

Table arrangements

You are born with energy, but you need to replenish it as you live. In traditional Chinese medicine, there are two principal sources for this "post-natal Chi". One is the air we breathe and the other is food and drink. Nutrition and the conditions in which we ingest it are considered absolutely vital to a long, healthy life. In the world of Feng Shui this understanding extends to the way in which we decorate our dining tables and arrange

people around them. For example, the colors we use are themselves sources of vibrating energy. Appropriately chosen table cloths and napkins can increase our appetite and support our digestive processes. Experiment with the advice on these pages at home, and the next time you go out to eat pay attention to the choices of colors and the mood they create in the restaurant.

Greens and blues
Green is for Wood and blue is for Water in the system of The Five Energies. They are cool tones and tend to reduce our appetites. You might consider using them for a light afternoon tea.

Reds and yellows
These are the colors of the Fire and Earth energies. Earth colors (yellows and browns) are perfectly harmonious with digestion. Fire (reds and oranges) is the mother of Earth and stimulates appetite. They are excellent on their own or in combination.

Golds and pinks
These are warm shades, also linked to Earth and Fire energies. They have a stimulating effect and generally tend to create a happy, convivial atmosphere, though not as intense as, for example, the red table cloths of a lively Italian café.

The whole earth

Your dining table is rather like a small planet of its own. It is like our earth, capable of accepting everything upon it and nourishing all those it supports. In that way, the table represents Earth energy. Wood is its grandparent (see pages 10–11), making wooden tables and yellowy-brown tones most appropriate. Then, as on earth, all the other energies are welcome. On this table (above) there are red and green (Wood) place mats and napkins, a glass (Earth) decanter of wine (Water), and cutlery (Metal). Overhead is the candelabra (Fire). No single energy predominates. This is a great asset in a harmonious setting.

Dinner for two

You are planning a romantic evening for two. The accumulated instincts of centuries will probably tell you how best to arrange the table, and a little Feng Shui advice may confirm this. Fire energy should be present, but not too intense. Try a table cloth in the purple spectrum. Candlelight will make a big difference, but use a single candlestick (in this case such Feng Shui advice takes precedence over the numbers recommended for you in your Ba Kua). Other energies are present on the table – Wood (the flowers), Water (the champagne), Earth (the plates and the table itself). Open your heart and enjoy.

Bathroom principles

The bathroom holds Water energy in your home. This unsteady energy pattern needs to be contained. Since it is also an area of the home where we dispose of waste and wash off accumulated dirt, it is best to locate the bathroom/toilet area separately from other rooms and keep the door closed, like a lid on a container.

Often when you are washing or using the bathroom/toilet you have a feeling of vulnerability. The very nature of Water energy is disturbing and mysterious. It is all the more important to think about how you are positioned in the bathroom/toilet, since your intuitive sense of personal security will be affected by this. You can use your Feng Shui view finder to help you. For example, if you are using the bathroom/toilet, is your back exposed? Are you vulnerable to sudden bursts of energy coming in if the door is opened unexpectedly? Do you have a clear phoenix aspect or do you feel somehow cut off by a wall that is very close to you?

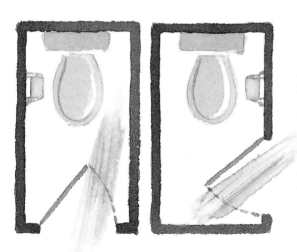

Placing the bathroom/toilet in a small area is always a problem. Try to ensure that the door does not open directly opposite, but is slightly out of the line of entry. This has been achieved in the layout shown above.

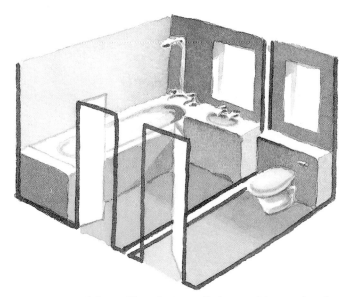

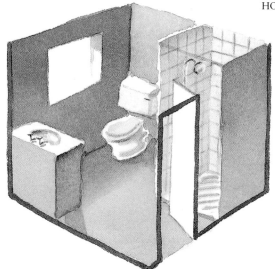

In normal Feng Shui design, all the washing and toilet facilities would be together in one room in order to contain the Water energy in that area. But you may want to subdivide the room into two, particularly if you have a large family and need to separate the toilet from the rest of the bathroom facilities to ease morning traffic jams in your home.

This is a good use of the space. The toilet is arranged in accordance with the Five Animals and the high shower cabinet is on the dragon side of the room itself. The energy flow in the room would be calmer if there were a blind on the window.

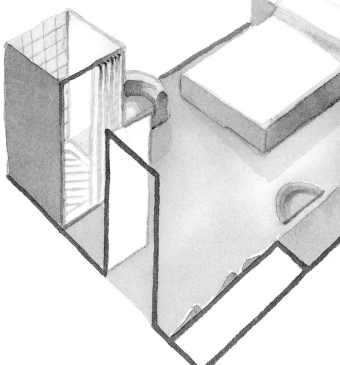

If you take your view finder to bed with you in this room, you will immediately see that you have a good tortoise, dragon and tiger, but there are several problems. The door opens almost opposite the foot of the bed and the shower cabinet is in front of you. Both interfere with your phoenix aspect. In addition, having water energy in your bedroom goes against a fundamental principle of Feng Shui.

113

Gardens

Your garden is a living field of energy and its power affects your home in many ways. We know this intuitively. When we visit a friend's home just think how often we take a quick look around the front room or the ground floor, but find ourselves wanting to look outside to see if there is a garden. Before we exclaim, "Ah, what splendid roses!" or make any other remarks about what we see, there is a brief moment in which we just naturally sense the energy, or the feel, of the garden – as if we were in the presence of another living being.

The power of gardens has been appreciated in China for centuries and their design has developed using a variety of elements, such as plant life, rock formations, and architectual elements, just as garden designers have done in other cultures. There are also basic Feng Shui principles that govern the fundamentals of garden layout. These can be applied to greenhouses as well.

The arrangement of the interior of your greenhouse will work best if it follows the fundamental Feng Shui design. The phoenix aspect is towards the door, so that area should be clear. The tortoise is the back of the interior with the dragon to the left and the tiger to the right.

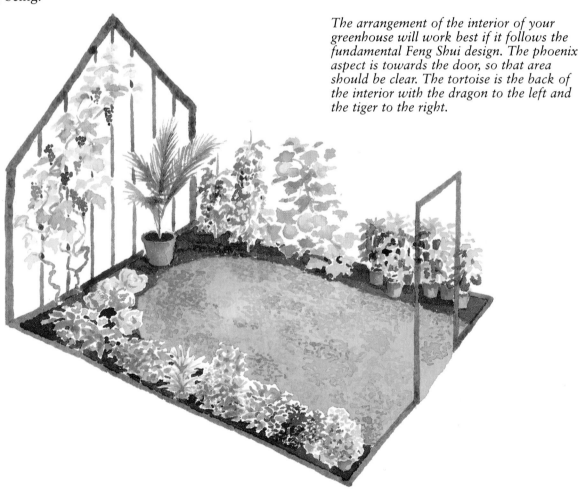

You can use your Feng Shui view finder in relation to your garden by facing the garden as you see it from your home. If you have a back garden, face it from the back of your home. If it is in front or to the side, face it from your front door or the entry point on the side. In this picture, the garden conforms to the basic Feng Shui principles, with the higher bushes and trees on the dragon side, the lower shrubs on the tiger side, and a clear view through to the distant phoenix.

The water rule

Feng Shui does not normally have fixed rules. It is based on principles which are applied in varying situations. This is why the best results are always achieved by seeking the advice of a Feng Shui master. However, it is almost always the case that you will be told not to have a body of water at the rear of your home. You should treat that as a rule. Only have water there if advised by a highly qualified practitioner.

This rule strikes many people as odd since it is so common to have fish ponds in gardens or swimming pools out the back. Sometimes the very idea of not having a pond or pool there makes people annoyed because their pond is a lovely part of their ornamental garden or because their swimming pool, installed at great expense, is an important part of family life.

The basis for the Feng Shui advice is that Water is one of the least stable of The Five Energies. It is regarded as "the abyss", a source of profound danger in the *I Ching*. If it is at the back of your home, it renders your essential tortoise aspect almost powerless. The surface of the pool or pond acts like a random mirror, intensifying and bouncing incoming energies all around the rear of your home. If you have a pool and can't move it, the best remedy is to keep it covered when not in use.

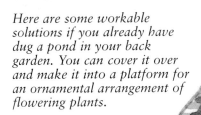

Here are some workable solutions if you already have dug a pond in your back garden. You can cover it over and make it into a platform for an ornamental arrangement of flowering plants.

If you have children, you can turn the pond into a sandpit, so that you still have a recreational area in your garden, but one that poses no dangers to the energies surrounding your home.

You can fill in the pond, and design areas of brick or stone work as borders around shrubs and bushes, adding attractive ground cover.

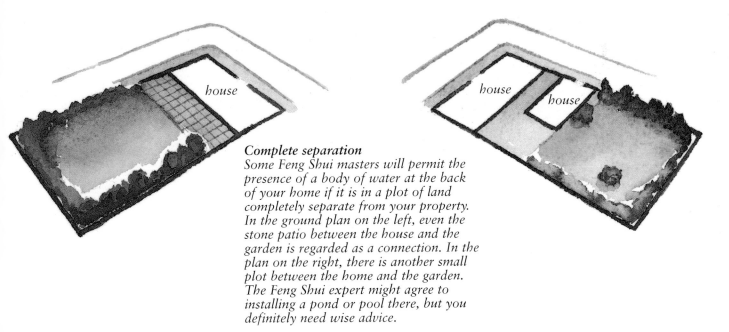

Complete separation
Some Feng Shui masters will permit the presence of a body of water at the back of your home if it is in a plot of land completely separate from your property. In the ground plan on the left, even the stone patio between the house and the garden is regarded as a connection. In the plan on the right, there is another small plot between the home and the garden. The Feng Shui expert might agree to installing a pond or pool there, but you definitely need wise advice.

Public squares

It is not by accident that advertisers are keen to
dominate so many of the world's public squares.
Throughout the centuries, these vast open spaces have
been focal points for the energy of nations. The traces
of automobile tail lights evoke the constant swirl of
energy around London's Piccadilly Circus, whose
curves are echoed by the buildings that surround it.
The legendary Eros memorial fountain attracts energy
into the square, still drawing people to its magnetism
late at night.

Energy snakes through Times Square in downtown Manhattan (left), creating a constant hustle and bustle. This is no place to have a quiet, calm apartment. But it is perfect for enterprises that thrive on constant movement and excitement. The neon lights tell the story: theatres, cinemas, video shops, and take-away fast food joints. Everyone is welcome to pass through. At night it is filled with milling crowds, theatregoers, and people entering and leaving its restaurants and bars. It is a river of energy: thousands have thronged to this "crossroads of the world" on election nights, at the ends of wars, and to welcome the New Year.

The Trevi Fountain in Rome (right) and its breathtaking backdrop ensure that this is one of the world's best-known squares. Like all great fountains, the streams of water and the pool attract and trap energy. People are pulled towards these powerful "energy spots" like metallic dust to a magnet. The sculptured edifice itself conforms to one of the most important Feng Shui principles by creating in front of itself a spacious vista overlooking a body of water.

Tiger homes

Your car is a tiger. From the Feng Shui point of view it has many of the most important characteristics of this extraordinary animal. It has immense power and can spring into action at a moment's notice, reaching high speeds within seconds. It is low, with a firm body which moves close to the ground. Even when still, it conveys a feeling of tremendous power and commands respect. Perhaps you even think of your car purring or roaring, but either way you have a underlying appreciation of its feline qualities.

Tiger on the right side
If you have a garage or a carport, the best place for it is on the side of your house that corresponds to the tiger position. As you face outwards from the front door, your garage should be next to or against the right side of the building.

Garage design

No part of the home escapes the notice of the Feng Shui
expert. The way you lay out the interior of your garage
makes a difference, too. There is no point in having an area
of disturbed energy right next to your house. Many people
use the garage as an external storage area for all sorts of
equipment and supplies they don't want to keep in their
home. Put up shelving along the dragon side of the garage.
This will be on the left as you face outwards. Put solid, heavy
items for long-term storage along the back wall, to strengthen
the tortoise. Bicycles, lawnmowers, and other appliances on
wheels can go along the tiger side.

Office energy

Feng Shui is commonly used in the business sector. In Hong Kong and Taiwan, where Feng Shui is widely practiced, most businesses will call in a Feng Shui master to give advice on the building of a new office. But it is not only in the selection of the location and the design of the building that Feng Shui can help. The time you spend in the office forms a major part of your life. Following the advice outlined in this book can have a positive effect on your health and wellbeing in the office. It may also improve your productivity and career prospects, and lead to greater profits for the organization for which you work.

You can use Feng Shui in your own office to determine the best location of your desk and the best direction to face when sitting. You can use its principles to determine the most suitable position to occupy in conferences or meeting rooms. In today's businesses, many major decisions are taken in a conference room – decisions that can affect your future or the future of the company. Therefore, if you are giving a presentation, and you use Feng Shui to position yourself in the best possible space, then you will give yourself a most definite advantage.

The structure of a meeting room is unusual in that there is usually only one entrance or exit, and often the windows (if there are any) have the blinds pulled. In this type of contained space, energy flowing into the room will behave like sound vibrations emanating from a hi-fi speaker. The energy coming into the room will bounce around like a billiard ball and then, as it becomes less powerful, begin to spiral round the room and back out through the door.

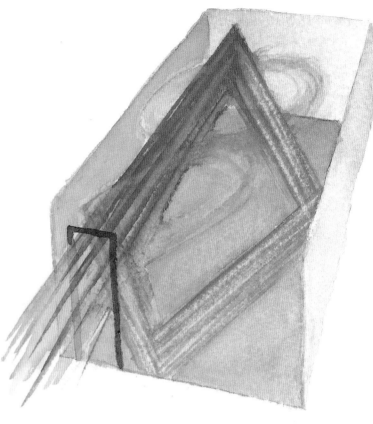

The energy flows
This is how a Feng Shui master sees the energy flowing in and around typical meeting rooms. Understanding these movements of energy is the starting point for finding the most harmonious locations. As energy enters these spaces it is very strong, but dissipates as it travels around the rooms. Working while sitting in the full force of the energy can make you confused or agitated. On the other hand, your mind will become dull if you sit in an area that receives almost no energy and is virtually stagnant. The best position will be the one that receives the energy like a gentle breeze to keep you refreshed and alert.

Worst places, best seats

Compare the layouts of these meeting rooms with the patterns of energy shown entering and moving around the same spaces on pages 122–3. You can see how certain places will be directly in the path of strong incoming energy while others will be less affected by it. For example, if you choose the dark chair immediately in line with the door (right) you will be buffeted by the incoming strong energy. This will attack your tiger side and make you uneasy and irritable. The best position is in the light chair, because it does not take the full force of the energy entering the room. If you sit here you will have a solid wall behind for the tortoise position, empty space in front for the phoenix aspect with a good view of people arriving or leaving, and strong dragon and tiger sides.

Door forces
In this room, the two people in the dark chairs are directly exposed to the energy from the door. The one sitting with their back to the door is attacked from the rear, destabilizing their tortoise. The other person experiences energy disturbing their phoenix aspect.

The light chairs are in more harmonious locations. The one on the right has a weak dragon side since it is punctuated by the door, but has a strong tiger side. That would be preferable for a woman since the tiger is regarded as female in Feng Shui. The one on the left, with its strong dragon, would be better for a man, since the dragon is seen as male.

Cross current
The person sitting in the dark chair (left) will be constantly distracted by having the door immediately next to them. They will have difficulty in coping with the full force of the energy streaming across them. The person opposite them at the far end of the table will be much more comfortable and able to concentrate better. You can see the reason for this by examining the energy flows shown for this same room on page 123. The person at the far end of the room is sitting in a much more gentle stream of energy. They have a solid wall at their back and plenty of space for their phoenix aspect.

Odd spaces
Many office buildings have small, irregularly shaped meeting rooms. In this one (right), the most vulnerable position is directly in the path of incoming energy, which also affects people on that side of the table. More favourable positions are on the other side. The chair with its back to the door is also unsuitable, since whoever sits there for the duration of the meeting will be subject to the sub-conscious nervousness that results from having a weak tortoise at the rear.

125

Downtown inferno

Most modern offices network their computers so that the employees can readily share information, use electronic mail, and access the Internet. To provide this facility, the computer is connected to the network by a cable. Usually, cables run under the floor from wiring closets to every computer in the office.

All electrical items, including power leads, network cables, and lighting, have electric and magnetic fields associated with them. Everyone in the office is surrounded by these fields. They come from a variety of sources, including the wiring for power, phone and network cables, fluorescent lighting, computers, and the air conditioning.

Some fields may be of low power, but even these add up to an environment of energetic disturbance that can negatively affect the health of people who work in it for sustained periods of time.

In the system of The Five Energies, electricity and electronic equipment like computers are considered to be Fire energy. In traditional Chinese medical theory, a serious imbalance of Fire energy affects the heart and disturbs the nervous system. The results of prolonged exposure to the upward force and intense power of Fire energy can affect your concentration. It can lead to headaches, anxiety, and loss of sexual appetite. You find you are nervous, jumpy, and unable to relax.

If you work in this type of office, you will always be using up your own energy as your system tries to cope with the excess Fire energy that envelops you. This in turn weakens your immune system, and therefore your resistance to disease.

Depending on circumstances, there may be methods to counteract the affects of these electromagnetic fields. Some businesses call in a Feng Shui expert to determine how and what may be done.

But if your company is not alert to this problem and you find yourself spending long hours working in such an environment, you should take as many breaks as possible to get out of the disturbing energy fields. Literally go outside the building when you are taking a break. Stand in the open air. To cool your inner Fire disturbance, drink bottled water that you purchase and consume outside the building. Always take your full allotment of holidays. Practice relaxation exercises to help calm your nervous system. Systems like Chi Kung, if taught by a qualified teacher, will help you replenish your lost energy and rebalance your system.

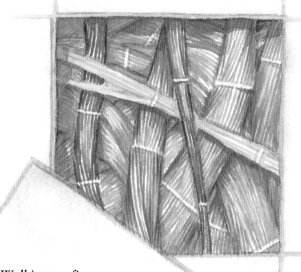

Walking on fire
Lift the floor tiles in a typical modern office and you find that you are spending your days sitting or walking over streams of electrical cable. Each radiates its own electromagnetic field, as do the banks of computers, TV screens, and telecommunications facilities. You are literally surrounded by Fire energy.

Facing forward

In an office like this one, where would you sit if you had a choice? Increasingly, office design is open plan. This can make room for flexibility, but often ends up supplying staff with modular seating arrangements that contradict Feng Shui principles. Many work stations require the person to sit facing a partition. This can be efficiently used for shelving and notice board space. However, if you sit facing the partition, you may end up with your back (tortoise) exposed to open space, while the partition cuts off your phoenix aspect. If you are sitting like this, you are like the little child facing the wall (see page 93). Your Feng Shui view finder will immediately alert you that it is one of the least satisfactory arrangements possible.

Turning outward
The two people in the work stations (below right) have no phoenix aspects. Their vision is literally cut off and their creativity will suffer. The best thing for them to do is turn 90 degrees so that they are facing outward at right angles to the partition. The nearest person will be at an advantage, having the tall partition on their left, the dragon side.

Face to face
The two desks above left have no partition. This is much better from the Feng Shui point of view, but it does mean that the two people spend much of their day facing each other directly. If they are compatible, fine. If not, then the desks could be turned back to back, with a partition between the two chairs.

Manager's viewpoint
A Feng Shui expert would recommend that managers have separate offices. However, if open plan is the only option, the corner area (left) could be suitable. The manager would need to ensure that they are facing outwards and not staring at the partition. They would then have a better view of most of the office to monitor and manage the department's progress. By closing the window behind them and having the blind always down, their tortoise side will be stronger.

Finding your direction
When you try to secure a good location in an office like this, first use your Feng Shui view finder, concentrating on having a solid tortoise and an open phoenix aspect. But, if that is not possible (below), then see if you can sit so that you are facing your best direction. This is the direction first listed in the explanation that accompanies your Ba Kua (pages 66–83).

129

Entrances and receptions

The entrance and reception area of an office block or other similar building needs to be well-positioned and properly designed to bring good fortune to all those who use it and occupy it. The function of the reception area is considered extremely important in Feng Shui, as it controls the flow of energy in and out of the building. A properly arranged reception area will help keep the flow of energy steady and harmonious.

Warm welcomes
The look and feel of the reception area is extremely important. It gives your clients and visitors one of their first impressions of you and often provides them with their first point of contact with your business, staff, and organizational culture. It is of supreme importance to make your visitors feel warmly welcome and at ease.

The architect of this building (right) has created a specially furnished waiting area slightly separated from the reception desk so that visitors can take it easy before being collected by the staff member they are meeting. Wherever they sit, they will have a solid tortoise on the rear, dragons and tigers to either side, and ample space for their phoenix in front. The door has been skilfully angled so that neither the receptionist nor the visitors face gusts of strong energy coming directly at them.

Separate and secure
The receptionist should be attentive to your visitors and not be forced to spend undue time on the telephone. This is discourteous, distracts from the running of an efficient switchboard, and is not effective if you expect the receptionist to play a role in maintaining security on the premises. A Feng Shui expert would normally advise you to separate the functions of the reception and the switchboard, and to locate the switchboard away from the reception area.

Wise advice
A wise business makes a good investment in a well-designed reception area. Decorations and furnishings should convey the image of the company at its best. Good reception facilities will lift staff morale and affect the way the reception staff respond to everyone who enters. Some corporations seek advice from a Feng Shui master especially for this aspect of their buildings. Investing heavily in the proper arrangements at the entrance to your building is, from the Feng Shui point of view, of far greater importance than lavishly decorating your corridors and meeting rooms.

Feng Shui interviews

You can use Feng Shui principles whether you are looking for a job or trying to employ someone to work for you. In countries where Feng Shui is widely used, this is common and it would be no surprise to anyone if a member of an interview panel were to refer to some aspect of Feng Shui in making a decision about whom to appoint to a particular job.

Supposing you are a senior executive and you are hoping to employ a reliable middle manager in a department of your company that has had many personnel problems. You are looking for a good leader, with excellent interpersonal skills. There are four candidates to interview, all with comparable levels of experience and ability.

The rest of the interview panel seems to favour a man in his forties with stamina, a solid track record of seeing tasks through to completion, and a personal style that is modest and non-aggressive. You check his date of birth: 2 February 1955. He was born in the Year of the Sheep. His stamina, durability, and modesty fit with this. But sheep are not leaders. They take the burdens on themselves; they don't transform situations. You look to see if there is anyone else among the candidates of equivalent competence who is likely to display strong leadership capability.

Using your knowledge of the Zodiac in this way does not mean that you automatically discriminate against people because of their year of birth. It means that you can add a further dimension to all the factors that you take into account in making the right selection, in the best interests both of that person and of your company and its workforce. For example, to be fair to all candidates, you might ask each one specific questions about their previous work to see if they conform to the underlying

patterns attributed to them in the Zodiac – and to see how compatible they would be in the particular job you are offering.

Preparing for an interview

If you are looking for a job, you might first decide whether you really want to work for the particular company which is advertising to fill a vacancy. Without the benefit of Feng Shui, you might just ask around to see what you can find out about the company. But, using this book and *The Feng Shui Handbook*, you could learn a lot about the company and its prospects by making a discreet survey of the

company's location. Is it situated in a building which conforms to Feng Shui principles? You can use your Feng Shui view finder or the Five Animals system to examine this. For example, does the front of the building have any open space in front or is it blocked off by another office tower? You can look at the roads, shopping areas, and other offices in the area to see if they are prospering or in decline. Also, take a good look at the reception area (see pages 130–1). This is the face of the company. How does it treat its visitors and its own staff?

Perhaps you can arrange to see the place where you would actually be working. You will be spending many hours of your life in that spot, so it could be well worth your time to see what you are getting into. If you will be working in a high-tech office, you could check to see if there are any open spaces or cafés nearby where you can go for a quick break during the day.

To improve your success during the interview you should deploy all the knowledge you have managed to glean from this book. Begin with the Zodiac. Which animal are you and which of your inner strengths are likely to be your best asset in this job? Think about how to convey that during the interview. On reflection, you might decide that you are not well suited to this particular type of work – and decide to find opportunities better suited to your real strengths.

Take into account the information you have about your trigram from the *I Ching*. What are the colors that most strongly support your own energy pattern? Can you find a way to wear those colors, even as an accent on a scarf or tie?

Be clear in your mind about how to use your Feng Shui view finder. For example, in the interview room below, the panel is sitting directly opposite the door and the candidate is forced to sit facing them. If you found yourself in a similar situation, you could at least adjust your chair when you sat down so that it was a few degrees to the left or right. You might put it on a very slight angle so that your back was oriented towards the corner, rather than the door. Your posture and manner of sitting would become naturally more relaxed and less like a prisoner before a row of judges.

Public buildings

A building, like a person, needs support. In the Feng Shui world, this comes not only from the earth, but from surrounding structures – a higher structure to the rear, a slightly taller building on the left, a somewhat lower edifice to the right, with unobstructed open space in front. A lonely tower, like this bank facing the Plaza de Catalunya in Barcelona (below), lacks all-round protection and is exposed to incoming energies on all sides. The little towers on the wing may accentuate the possibility of internal conflict.

The circular front surrounding the main entrance of the town hall in the German city of Bielefeld (right) has a powerful effect on the energy that surrounds it. The sweeping curve attracts strong bands of energy, making this site a particularly potent focal point in the life of the community. The sharp concrete angle that faces the camera may have a beneficial, protective effect on the town hall itself, but like a fully drawn bow, it shoots an invisible stream of sharp energy straight out towards whatever is opposite.

The Stock Exchange in Sydney
(below) is a fine example of
Feng Shui principles at work. Its
entrance is subtly balanced and
quietly conveys a feeling of
enduring stability. The dark
stone planters on either side of
the main steps leading to the
entrance lend silent weight and
solidity to the entire structure.
The leafy tree which rises to the
left of the entrance stretches up
slightly higher than its
companion on the right, a
perfect balance of the dragon
and tiger. The curving façade
attracts power to the whole
building and the design evokes
the feeling of a human mouth
opening wide to receive the
energy perpetually arriving at
its portals.

135

Leading positions

Producing the best results from team work or getting the best possible decision out of a meeting is one of the most difficult tasks facing any chief executive. Whether you are the president, the chair of the board, or the managing director of your firm or institution, you need all the support you can get. Feng Shui principles can be applied here, too – not only for your own benefit, but for the cohesiveness of everyone who is working with you.

The boardrooms on these pages have both been arranged so as to place the person chairing the meeting in positions that create strong fields of energy around them. This helps them conduct the meeting with the necessary authority and to focus the energies of the other people in the room.

You can also look back to the pages on Power seating and From stools to armchairs (pages 94–7) to see what sort of furniture is most appropriate for the person running the meeting. It is not accidental that so many corporations and other bodies reserve one chair in particular for the chief executive, usually one that is slightly larger than the others, with a higher back and with solid arms on either side. An extreme example of this is found in court rooms the world over where the presiding judge frequently has a chair that is larger and raised slightly higher than the rest of the court, even higher than any associate members of the judiciary.

There should be a solid wall directly behind the chair. Any trophies and emblems should be placed near the door, the most appropriate place for Metal energy in the room and to remind people of the institution's successes when they enter and leave.

Using the circle
Some companies, particularly in the Orient, will use a circular table and arrange the seating so that the chief executive, or the person chairing the meeting, can sit facing his or her most auspicious direction. You can establish your own position from the explanation that accompanies your Ba Kua. It will be the first direction listed. In the room above, the person who will chair the meeting has the Ba Kua for Thunder (see pages 74–5) and so the seat has been placed to face East.

IN
YOUR
WORKPLACE

Perfect positioning
*Behind the president's chair a solid
wall provides a powerful tortoise. On
the wall to the left of the chair a high
bookcase makes a lofty dragon. Beside
the wall to the right stands a lower
serving table, the correct position for
the tiger. At the far end of the room,
floor-to-ceiling windows enable the
president's phoenix to fly far ahead.*

Making presentations

Your company asks you to make a sales presentation at the offices of a potential new client. It is a major project, and since the client is part of an international network, possibilities for worldwide sales may open up. You are confident about your product and your presentation has worked well before. But in most cases, the prospective clients came to your offices and you felt comfortable making your pitch in known surroundings.

This is precisely when your Feng Shui view finder and the other information in this book will come to your aid. Ask if you could see the room in which you will be making the

presentation a day or so before. If that is not possible, ask if you could see it an hour or so before the meeting. Use that time to study the room. Think about the movements of energy, examining the location of the doors and windows. Then, use your Feng Shui view finder to choose the situation that will be most advantageous for you. Does the furniture need to be rearranged in any way? Don't be hesitant about doing this. If necessary you can explain that your past experience has shown that people follow the presentation more closely if the environment enables them to concentrate better.

Improve your pitch

A good position in the room helps to keep you bright and alert, and projects positive energy. A client comes to your offices for a sales meeting (left). You are keen to get a firm order from his company. Put yourself in the best possible position. Assess the energy movement in the room using the information on pages 122–3. Make sure you are not in a direct line with the door or in a stagnant area of the room. Use your Feng Shui view finder to ensure that all your animals are in the correct relationship to each other and rearrange the furniture in the room if necessary.

Smart position

Your position in the room has a subtle, but often decisive, effect on the impact of your presentation. Just imagine if you were to give a major presentation jammed up beside the door or from a point where people could not see your charts.

The Feng Shui advice is to use your view finder. Make sure you have reasonably good backing such as a wall or partition – not open windows, windows without blinds, or a large empty space. Have a good clear view of everyone in front of you. You can judge their reactions and they can focus on you. Have your tall display charts or easel to your left, your dragon side. If you have equipment or a side table, have it on your right, your tiger side.

139

Eating out

Sometimes you peer through the window of a restaurant and you just know that you don't want to eat there. It is nothing to do with the food, or even the people inside. You just have the feeling that you don't like the atmosphere. This may be your intuition, but it may also be your own innate understanding of some of the fundamental principles of Feng Shui. Once you are familiar with your Feng Shui view finder, start using it to assess the arrangements in various types of restaurant – or, once inside, to pick the table you would prefer.

Private nooks
Some older restaurants still keep back-to-back seating arrangements and you can find contemporary variations on it in diners, fast food restaurants, and some bars. This kind of seating makes everyone feel remarkably secure, and no wonder – everyone gets a very strong tortoise at their back. The people who sit with their backs to the farthest wall have an even stronger sense of this power because they are backed by the tortoise of the restaurant itself. This kind of seating is excellent for intimate conversations or private business discussions. Each group is relatively secluded in its own booth. Since each person's phoenix aspect is compressed and overlaps with that of the person opposite, people naturally focus on each other and there is an automatic mingling of the fields of attention.

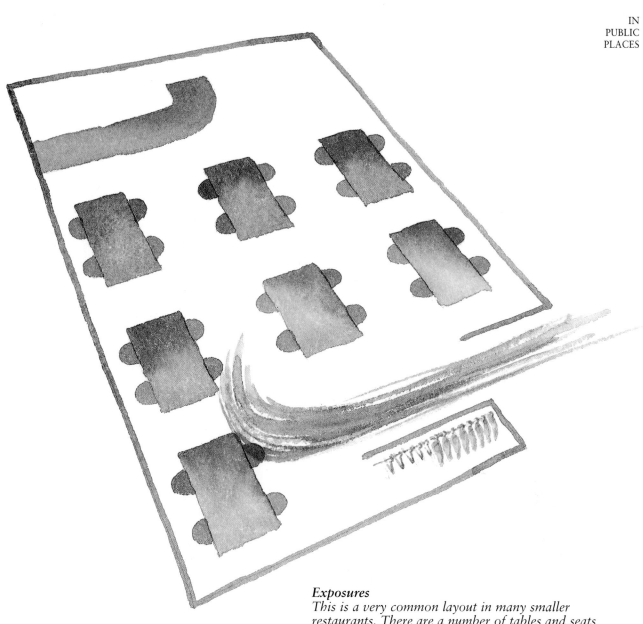

Exposures
*This is a very common layout in many smaller
restaurants. There are a number of tables and seats
that you would avoid. First of all, the seat directly
in line with the door exposes you to all manner of
incoming energies, whether you are facing it or,
worse, have your back to it. The seats against the
walls offer solid tortoises, but the majority of seats
have their backs exposed to the center of the
restaurant. If the restaurant was full, this would be
less of a problem since the backs of all the people
in the exposed chairs would provide tortoise shells
for each other.*

141

Backs and snacks

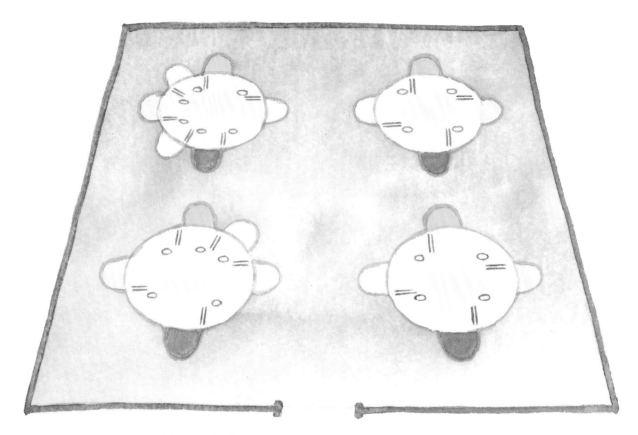

Chinese circles

When you study the arrangement of people around each of these circular tables, you will see why it is not surprising that many Chinese restaurants are organized according to this model. To begin with, when you sit round a circular table you always have someone on your right and left. This means that each person automatically has their own dragon and tiger.

The people in the yellow chairs have good tortoises – they have a wall directly behind them. Those in the green seats have the entire restaurant behind them supporting their tortoise. Even the people in the blue seats have a tortoise, because their backs are protected by the glass in the front window of the restaurant. The tortoises of the remaining seats benefit either from the chairs of the people immediately behind them or from a wall at a slight angle to their backs. In this way, the configuration of circles provides most customers with a reasonably good Feng Shui position.

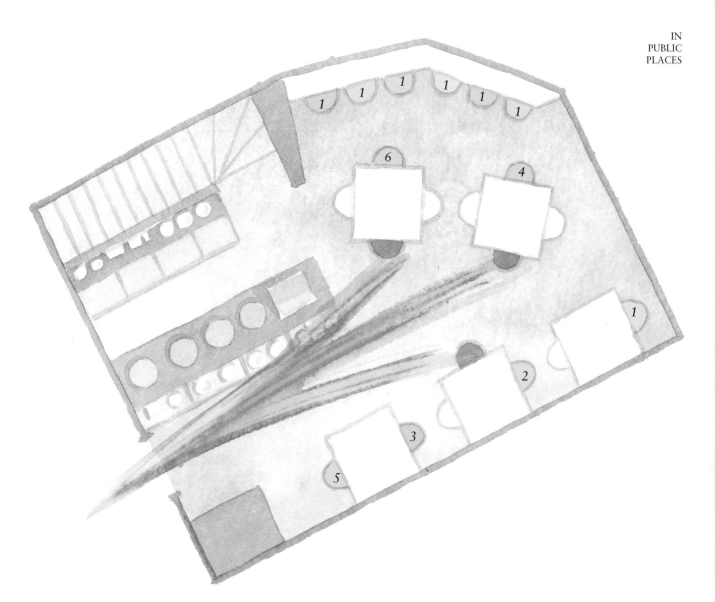

Snack bar animals

You pop in to a busy snack bar for a quick sandwich and a coffee. Even in the rush of the day, it is wise to find a location where your nervous system can settle down and take a break. If you can only find a space at the wall counter, sit sideways so that your phoenix is not cut off by the wall in front of you. The best seats are marked in gold, since they have the best tortoises. The numbers indicate the order of preference. The other positions in the bar are more vulnerable. The worst locations are marked in blue. Business will be brisk in this particular bar because the door opens towards the dragon side of the space, which is always more welcoming. On the other hand, all the staff work behind the counter on the tiger side, which means that they will be more likely to argue among themselves unless other measures are taken to calm the energy on that side.

Cinemas and theatres

You enter a cinema just before the movie starts. You see rows and rows of seats ranged in front of you. Sometimes you have an eerie feeling, almost as if you were completely exposed to unknown forces. Where do you decide to sit?

Perhaps you have the same feeling when the person at the theatre box office asks you if you have a preference for seating.

Of course, you cannot always get the seats you want, but from a Feng Shui point of view it is clear which seats are the best in the house. These seats may not necessarily be the most expensive and the advice might not go along with your normal habits and preferences. But it could be worth trying, especially if you are a person who genuinely experiences uncertainty when faced with the unpredictable space inside a theatre or cinema.

The three drawings on the facing page enable you to see how energy circulates inside the space of three very different cinemas and theatres. Just as in your home, office, or a meeting room, this is the starting point for determining the seats in which you will feel most comfortable and secure.

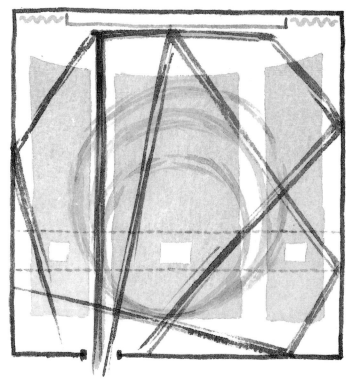

Arrows and circles

In this cinema (left), two streams of energy arrive through the back entrance. One is straight and sharp, like the flight path of an arrow. The other is curved and more gentle, like flowing water. The arrow-like energy streams towards the screen, some of it bouncing back to the left, some towards the right, and some of it sliding along the screen before heading back out to the right-hand wall.

The slower-moving energy begins to make a series of widening circles until it has moved around the space and begun to flow back towards the original entrance. These two patterns leave certain areas surrounded by energy, but not attacked by it. This helps to determine the most suitable seating (see pages 146–7).

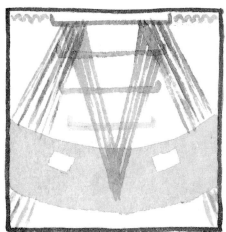

Balconies

The energy that flows towards the stage in this theatre (above left) from the audience naturally bounces back out, and as it moves towards the curved balconies, it converges on the center. Avoid sitting directly in the center seats and choose seats slightly back from the front row.

In the round

Energy passes down the aisles of this theatre-in-the-round (above right), so you would normally avoid seats on either side of the passageways. Otherwise, it circulates calmly around the space and you can choose a seat anywhere.

Theatre seating

In a cinema or theatre with no central aisle, whether you are on the ground floor level or in a balcony, think of the entire space in accordance with your Feng Shui view finder. Your back should be near a solid wall or partition, you should have a wide open expanse in front of you, and you should benefit from equal protection on both your right and left sides. So the best seat is in the center towards the rear back row. You might prefer the very back if the seats are against the wall or a partition. If the seats are separated from the back wall, sit three or four rows in from the back, to allow the rear rows to give you that protection. Even if the rows are empty, your position is still fine since any people who arrive there will sit down and the currents behind you will be less disturbed.

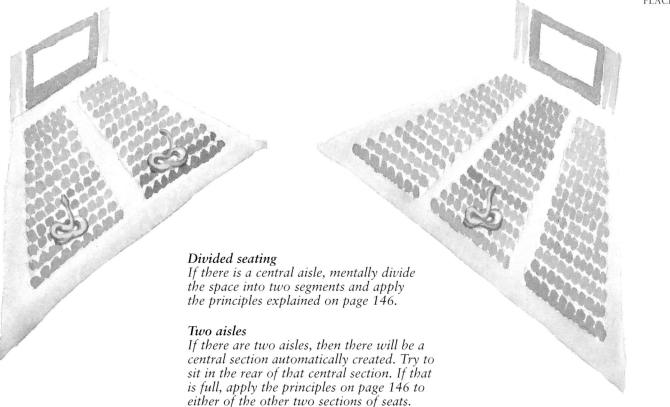

Divided seating
If there is a central aisle, mentally divide the space into two segments and apply the principles explained on page 146.

Two aisles
If there are two aisles, then there will be a central section automatically created. Try to sit in the rear of that central section. If that is full, apply the principles on page 146 to either of the other two sections of seats.

The box in the theatre

Theatre boxes are often associated with nobility, high-ranking officials, or wealthy personalities. But no matter how distinguished he might be, a Feng Shui master would not ask to sit there. Half the phoenix aspect is cut off because the box does not face the stage directly. Everyone in the box is vulnerable to any energy currents that might abruptly enter the box through the rear door (see right).

Standing room only

Stand in the middle of the section allocated for standing room. If you can put your back against the wall, that is ideal.

The assassination of President Abraham Lincoln, shot by John Wilkes Booth who entered his box in a Washington theatre in 1865.

147

On the move

Whether you drive alone or with passengers, don't forget your Feng Shui animals. Some aspects of the design of your car probably correspond to them perfectly. For example, you have your tiger under your right foot where you control both the forward power of your vehicle and also bring it to a halt.

If you are a passenger, the best seat to occupy from the Feng Shui point of view is the rear seat on the dragon side. The rear is preferable because of the strong support from the back seat which acts as your tortoise shell. You have a fuller interior view of the car from the back seat, so your phoenix is freer. The dragon side is always associated with stability and clarity rather than the right side, which has connotations of violence.

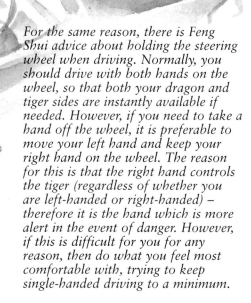

For the same reason, there is Feng Shui advice about holding the steering wheel when driving. Normally, you should drive with both hands on the wheel, so that both your dragon and tiger sides are instantly available if needed. However, if you need to take a hand off the wheel, it is preferable to move your left hand and keep your right hand on the wheel. The reason for this is that the right hand controls the tiger (regardless of whether you are left-handed or right-handed) – therefore it is the hand which is more alert in the event of danger. However, if this is difficult for you for any reason, then do what you feel most comfortable with, trying to keep single-handed driving to a minimum.

On the buses

Take your Feng Shui view finder on the
bus with you. Sit facing forward so that
your phoenix is flying in the same
direction as the movement of the bus. Try
to find a seat on the dragon side of the
bus, if possible. For safety sake, avoid
sitting too close to the front. You will
have a stronger tortoise if you sit towards
the rear, but not at the very back. An aisle
seat is preferable to a window seat,
because you are less vulnerable and can
exit more easily.

Urban rails

You may travel around your city in a
street car or tram, or use the subway or
underground. Or you may use a
monorail. Applying your Feng Shui view
finder to each of these systems, you
would normally try to find a seat facing
forward in the same direction that the
carriage is moving. If that is not possible,
try to sit so that there is strong support,
such as an armrest or a partition, to
restrain you if the carriage suddenly
stops. Normally, it is better to sit near an
exit, preferably one you can see.

Going by train

The Feng Shui advice is not to sit at the
front end of the train. The reason is
simple – if there is a serious accident the
greatest damage is usually in the first and
second carriages.

There can also be incidents involving
the rear carriages so it is prudent to avoid
these if possible and find seating in the
middle carriages. In the event of a crash,
there are usually far more survivors in
the middle part of the train.

Airports

The gracious design of the TWA
Terminal at New York's JFK airport
(above) is perfectly adapted to its
purpose. The sweeping lines of the
structure evoke the spirit of flight.
Each of the curves ensures a smooth
flow of energy around the structure,
just as the subtle curves of a bird's
wing enable it to soar through the air.

A Feng Shui master could have
warned the developers of the
new Denver International
Airport (above) to think twice
about this design. Before it
opened, the airport suffered a
series of calamities such as
cracking concrete and faults in
the baggage handling system.
   So intense was the debate
about the new building, that the
local newspaper, The Denver
Post, arranged for three Feng
Shui practitioners to offer
suggestions for healing the ailing
airport. Their main concern
focused on the white peaked
rooftop, despite the fascination
it prompted from the world of

The symmetrical layout of London Heathrow's Terminal Four is clearly seen in this aerial view (below). The figure-of-eight approach road coils in front of the main building in a series of continuous lazy curves which protect the space from incoming "sharp energy". The calm curves on either side of the central complex create pools of smooth-moving currents which bathe the building in a calm sea of energy.

professional architects. But what an airport needs is an environment which is calm, steady, and harmonious, both for the safety of arriving and departing aircraft and for all who use its facilities.

Even an untrained eye can see immediately that this is a roof which creates sharp upward movements of energy: imagine the patterns of air above the roof as the currents speed up and down the valleys, peaks, and spikes of the structure. The long line of points cuts through space like the sharpened teeth of a hand saw.

Phony Feng Shui

Feng Shui has become fashionable in certain parts of the Western world these days. You find more and more people advertising themselves as Feng Shui practitioners. Knowing whether you have found an authentic expert or not is extremely difficult, and many people are disillusioned after experiences with phony Feng Shui experts. The following story may help you avoid similar sad experiences.

Charles was a 34-year-old architect working in a small, successful firm in southern England. He had brought a great deal of enthusiasm and creativity to the company and was being considered for promotion as a possible partner. He had been married for four years and was now the father of two small children.

Like most architects, he was aware of Feng Shui; but, unlike most, he decided that it was worth getting a Feng Shui expert to study his home and suggest improvements. He found several names in a magazine article and contacted them. One demanded a fee that was more than double the others, although he was the only person who claimed to have studied Feng Shui in China. The second one had a fixed schedule of rates, spoke well, and described Feng Shui as "an intuitive science". The third one was very cheap, said the work would take only about an hour, and was unusually clear about the specific benefits.

Charles ruled out the cheapest estimate, relying on his normal business sense, was not prepared to pay the highest fee, and so settled on the one with the fixed rates.

This turned out to be an older man, Hugh, with a background in teaching, before a serious illness had changed his lifestyle. Charles rather expected to see some special Feng Shui equipment being produced, but Hugh told him: "Equipment is used to measure the material world. We have no need of this in Feng Shui."

Hugh went through Charles' home, pausing, looking intently, sometimes closing his eyes. After an hour, he summed up his advice. "Life in this home is too cold. You have growing children and they need greater warmth. All the windows that face the morning sun should be enlarged and that room should have strong yellows. Your front room needs structural adjustments: it should have a door facing east, for warmth and wealth. To do this, you will need to change the relationship with the adjacent dining room, probably by altering the wall between them."

This advice fitted with Hugh's own ideas. The cost of making the alterations would be high, but after a long discussion with his wife, and in the hope that these changes might affect his prospects for promotion, he decided to make them.

Then began the long wait for the good luck. It never came. The firm could not afford to increase its team of partners. Charles hid his disappointment. But his enthusiasm waned, his concentration wavered. He closed up in the evenings, staring at the television. The atmosphere affected the little children, and soon long mornings were taken up waiting at the doctor's with complaints of headaches, tummy upsets, and odd little fevers.

"It all began with that damned Feng Shui man," his wife said to him one night, breaking the silence after dinner.

This was the last thing that Charles wanted anyone to say to him, because he had harboured the same suspicion for months.

"We had to trust his training," said Charles limply, "just as people trust me because of my training."

"What training did he have?" she demanded. "You just turned our home over to a complete stranger and now we're trapped in something neither of us wants or understands."

Charles despaired. He knew something had gone dreadfully wrong, but he had no idea what. A week later, one of his firm's senior partners returned from a two-year assignment in Hong Kong. She had been pleased when Charles first joined the company, and called him into her office. "Charles, you're just not the man I knew before I went away. What has happened?"

"My luck has turned," he said and fell silent.

"You believe in Lady Luck, do you Charles?" she asked. "You should have been with me in Hong Kong. There I was, working in the head offices of one of the largest property development corporations in the Far East, and we could barely make a move without consulting the Feng Shui men."

Charles looked up. "That's what I did," he told her.

"You consulted a Feng Shui man?" she exclaimed.

Charles related the full story, frequently interrupted by her pointed questions. Then there was a long silence.

"There are lots of phonies, Charles, all claiming to be Feng Shui experts. They read the books, they attend workshops, they may even take a course. No doubt they see the value of Feng Shui and want to help other people, but good wishes are no substitute for serious training. And this is not a skill you learn overnight. The Feng Shui masters in the companies I dealt with were more highly regarded that all the architects put together. Their art is handed down from master to

student in an unbroken succession and the training takes up to thirty years."

"So what should I do," asked Charles, struggling with his emotions.

"If I were you I would start by asking around in the Chinese community – try the owner of a Chinese bookshop. Feng Shui is so deeply a part of their culture, that's where you have to begin. But whoever you find, don't be afraid to ask for their credentials. A real expert will tell you exactly who his master was, how long he studied, and what system he uses. But expect modesty. A real master will tell you he knows very little, even after decades of study."

"But what if I can't find a Chinese master?" ask Charles thinking of his own failed efforts.

"Well, supposing someone comes to your home – if they don't use the Chinese compass, the Lo Pan, something is wrong. And they should ask you details about the date and time of birth of everyone in the house. Then, after they go around, they will ask for some time to themselves, maybe a couple of hours, during which they make their complicated calculations. And, by the way, the real experts will not only tell you what changes to make, but the exact day and time on which to make them!"

"I'm losing heart," said Charles. "This is all too much like magic. I just wanted good advice for me and my family."

"Well, Charles, you've suffered the effect of bad advice. Imagine if you had benefited from the power of good advice. Some people say that Feng Shui is a form of magic and certainly the masters I met had something very special about them. A real professional is like that. It is worth paying for the very best quality – because the cost of correcting mistakes can be enormous."

Jade and crystal

In the midst of a swirling cosmos, our relationship to the Earth is a great source of stability. If we are anxious, fearful, or nervous, we can help calm our nerves by reconnecting with the powerful energy of the Earth.

To the ancients, the stable energy of the Earth was seen to be particularly manifest in jade. The minerals that we know by this common name are among the hardest in the world. The importance of jade in the culture of various peoples has often been used as a measure of their high standard of civilization. Excavations of Chinese tombs have unearthed evidence that members of the imperial family were buried in robes fashioned from small squares of carved and polished jade.

The use of jade in Chinese culture is linked to the powerful Earth energy which the mineral absorbs over the long period it takes to form. Because of this process, jade acts as a powerful antidote to disturbances of our nervous system. Chinese-speaking people the world over incorporate jade into necklaces, pendants, bracelets, and rings – all are regarded as special bodyguards. Gifts of jade are given to children at birth, and to older people as a sign of respect.

Feng Shui masters may also use jade as a method of harmonizing and stabilizing energy in people's homes. Principally, jade attracts or strengthens Earth energy in a dwelling. But, using the system of The Five Energies, they may select different colors of jade to attract additional aspects of the energy spectrum.

Natural crystal

The custom of employing jade has been supplemented in recent times by the increasing use of crystal. Genuine natural crystal is also strongly associated with Earth energy, although its ability to attract such energy is less powerful than that of jade. Nevertheless, an experienced Feng Shui practitioner can make use of natural crystal to adjust the energies in your home, and may recommend that you wear a pendant of a particular crystal.

The use of crystal in the world of Feng Shui is complex and must be applied in conjunction with all the other energetic forces that the Feng Shui master takes into account, whether it is being used to enhance your home, help treat a particular illness, or even stimulate the growth of plants in your greenhouse.

Natural crystal – a Feng Shui expert will never use artificial crystal – has the power to attract certain types of auspicious energy and to repel harmful energies. In this way, a crystal can act like the ancient pyramids whose intense, compacted Earth energy and triangular shapes served as conduits channelling energies from the galaxy to earth. To the Chinese scholars of Feng Shui, the Egyptian pyramids are known to this day as "immense crystals".

Many Chinese people have a complete set of jade figures depicting all the animals of the Zodiac. Each year they display the appropriate figure in their home, such as a jade ox (above). Some may place the animal for their year of birth permanently in a special location to attract favourable energy.

Master Lam Kam Chuen

Master Lam Kam Chuen has a worldwide reputation in the fields of Tai Chi, Chi Kung, Traditional Chinese Medicine, and Feng Shui.

Master Lam was born in Hong Kong shortly after the Second World War and at a very early age began training in Tai Chi Chuan, Choy Lee Fut, Northern Shaolin Kung Fu, and Iron Palm under masters such as Lung Tse Chung and Yim Sheung Mo (both of whom were disciples of Ku Yue Chang, known throughout China as "The King of Iron Palm").

He also undertook the painstaking study of Chi Kung, a system for the cultivation of internal energy in the body. His supreme teacher in this field, with whom he studied in Beijing, is Professor Yu Yong Nian, the world's leading authority whose Grand Master was the eminent Wang Xiang Zhai.

Master Lam is also a practitioner of Traditional Chinese Medicine, a qualified bonesetter, and herbalist. He came to the West in 1976, becoming the first Tai Chi instructor appointed to teach in the Inner London Education Authority. He now teaches and practices medicine at The Lam Clinic in London's Chinatown.

Following the widely acclaimed BBC series, *The Way of the Warrior*, Master Lam was invited to act as consultant to the sequel publication,

The Way of Harmony. This was followed by his ground-breaking work published by Gaia Books, *The Way of Energy*, introducing the Zhan Zhuang Chi Kung system of Standing Like a Tree. This is now available in many languages worldwide, as is his second book, *Step-by-Step Tai Chi*.

In 1995 in the UK he presented the 10-part Channel 4 TV series, *Stand Still – Be Fit*, now released as a Channel 4 video production.

Master Lam is a fully qualified practitioner of Feng Shui, and has been training in this art for most of his life. He has studied under four masters in Hong Kong and Taiwan, each of whom is an acknowledged master in specialized aspects of Feng Shui (see acknowledgments on facing page). His first book on this subject, *The Feng Shui Handbook*, is an international bestseller.

Feng Shui services

Master Lam offers several types of Feng Shui service. For any corporation, he will assess prospective properties and advise on their suitability, review architects' plans and models, inspect construction sites to supervise specific Feng Shui requirements, and provide an annual advisory service to make all the necessary adjustments in accordance with the changing energy fields around and inside the premises.

For any business which is relocating or choosing a new location he will make an on-site visit to advise on the suitability of a location. He will also advise on any measures which should be taken by the owners to ensure favourable energy in their premises.

For any home, he will examine the existing property, recommend all necessary changes (which may involve structural work inside or outside), give specific instructions for any alterations, and make in-depth recommendations covering a period of several years. For any individual or family which is experiencing difficulties after moving into a new home, such as breakdown in the family atmosphere, unexpected health problems, and so forth, he will examine the entire property and make recommendations which will neutralize the "sharp energy" which is causing the disharmony in the environment.

For any individual or family looking for a new home who have located possible properties, he will visit their preferred location to advise on its suitability.

Whether the advice is for business or home, those who seek Feng Shui advice treat it as a major investment in their future health and prosperity, just as they do first-class preventative medical care. The fees reflect this. These are not normally fixed rates, but depend on the nature of the property and the work to be done.

The video
This unique video presents the fundamental principles of *The Feng Shui Handbook* and *The Personal Feng Shui Manual*. Master Lam shows you how this wisdom can be applied in everyday practical settings, and gives you fresh insight into the mind of a Feng Shui expert as he examines the world around him.

For these services or video, contact Master Lam direct at 70 Shaftesbury Avenue, London WC1V 7DF. Telephone: (44) 0831 802 598 or (44) 171 287 2114. Fax: (44) 171 437 3118.

Author's acknowledgments

I would like to express my very deep appreciation to the four masters who have guided me in my efforts to understand the profound world of Feng Shui. Master Lau Sau Hong first introduced me to the inner arts of Chinese Culture when I was growing up in Hong Kong. Following that early experience I studied throughout the 1970s in Hong Kong under Master Lee Chuen Lun. I was then accepted as a student by Master Wang Chung Han in Taiwan and even more recently Master Ho Chiu Hong in Hong Kong has given me valuable guidance.

Over the years, my family has been of immense importance to me and I want to take this opportunity to thank my wife, Kai Sin, and my three sons, Tin Yun, Tin Yu, and Tin Hun. They have made it possible for me to practice the arts in which I was trained and to endeavour to open up for the West the ideas and traditions of the Chinese way to health and harmony.

This book would not have been possible without the sustained support of Gaia Books, particularly on the part of the Managing Director, Joss Pearson, the Managing Editor, Pip Morgan, and the Art Director, Patrick Nugent.

The people who so ably assisted me in the production of *The Feng Shui Handbook*, kindly agreed to work on this subsequent project. The design is the work of Bridget Morley who spent countless hours developing and supervising the meticulous artwork, which was done by Michael Posen. She worked closely with the staff at Aardvark Editorial, who were responsible for the typesetting, and arranged the photo selection in conjunction with Gill Smith.

My student, Richard Reoch, worked with me over many months as we evolved different ways of presenting the fundamental concepts and tools of Feng Shui so that they could be of benefit to all readers of this book. Steve Bowden, an expert in the field of information technology and also a student of mine, kindly volunteered to help us in this undertaking and generously assisted us throughout.

Index

Photo credits

ADAMS PICTURE LIBRARY, p.135; ARCAID, p.14 left (Jeremy Cockayne), p.15 (Richard Bryant), pp.134/5 (Richard Bryant), p.150 (Ezra Stoller), pp.150/1 (John Baker); BRIDGEMAN ART LIBRARY, p.154 (ORM59908) Recumbent buffalo, Chinese [jade], Oriental Museum, Durham University/Bridgeman Art Library, London; BRITISH MUSEUM, (Copyright The British Museum), pp.2, 18, 84; MARY EVANS PICTURE LIBRARY, p.147 (Courtesy of Mary Evans Picture Library); SCIENCE PHOTO LIBRARY, p.155 (Martin Land); TONY STONE IMAGES, p.119 bottom (John Lawrence), p.119 top (Hiroyuki Matsumoto); ZEFA PICTURES LTD, *The Stock Market*, pp.7, 8, 14 right, 118, 134, 151.

Publisher's acknowledgments

Gaia would like to thank Master Lam and his wife Kai Sin for their generous hospitality and the delicious food provided on the many occasions that the team met at the Immortals Restaurant, Shaftesbury Avenue during the production of this book. Thanks also to Lynn Bresler for her proofreading and the index.

Also by Master Lam Kam Chuen

FENG SHUI

HANDBOOK

How to Create a Healthier Living and Working Environment

From bedroom to boardroom to backyard, this complete practical guide is intended to meet the growing interest in healthy design. The *Feng Shui Handbook* includes:

- The history of the ancient Chinese art of placement, the centuries-old way of interpreting the natural forces in the environment

- Advice on choosing the location of your home or office, positioning your furniture, and the proper orientation of structural details such as doors and windows

- Interpretations of the Feng Shui energies of major buildings around the world, including the United Nations and the White House

This unique application of ancient Chinese wisdom to contemporary Western needs introduces the practical steps you can take to make your living and working environment more attuned to the life forces around you. Beautifully illustrated with photographs and easy-to-follow design options, the *Feng Shui Handbook* draws on timeless Chinese principles – such as yin and yang, the *I Ching*, and the five element theory – to help you understand the proper arrangement of home and workplace in harmony with constant life changes. It provides a fresh look at how an intimate knowledge of Feng Shui can fundamentally improve your health and well-being.

0-8050-4215-6 • $16.95 • Pb
160 pp • Full-color illustrations throughout
Available at All Bookstores

A Henry Holt Reference Book
Henry Holt and Company, Inc.
115 West 18th Street
New York, New York 1001